Emotional Intelligence

For the Authentic and Diverse Workplace

Denys Santos Blell

iUniverse, Inc.

New York   Bloomington

Emotional Intelligence
For the Authentic and Diverse Workplace

iUniverse books may be ordered through booksellers or by contacting:

iUniverse
1663 Liberty Drive
Bloomington, IN 47403
www.iuniverse.com
1-800-Authors (1-800-288-4677)

ISBN: 978-1-4502-7026-7 (sc)
ISBN: 978-1-4502-7027-4 (dj)
ISBN: 978-1-4502-7028-1 (ebook)

Library of Congress Control Number: 2010916921

Printed in the United States of America

iUniverse rev. date: 01/05/2011

To my wife, Dalia, and my daughters,
Mwenza, Zinzi and Zainab

On Commitment

"Until one is committed, there is hesitancy, the chance to draw back, always ineffectiveness. Concerning all acts of initiative (and creation) there is one elementary truth, the ignorance of which kills countless ideas and splendid plans: That the moment one definitely commits oneself then Providence moves too. All sorts of things occur to help one that would never otherwise have occurred. A whole stream of events issues from the decision, raising in one's favor all manner of unseen incidents and meetings and material assistance, which no man could have dreamed would have come his way. I have learned a deep respect for one of Goethe's couplets: "Whatever you can do, or dream you can, begin it. Boldness has genius power and magic in it."

—W. H. Murray
The Scottish Himalayan Expedition (1951)

Foreword

In this work, Denys Blell offers some steps that each of us can take to address the reality of an increasingly interconnected world, a world where we can no longer rely on geographical, political, and cultural boundaries for addressing differences. In fact, if differences did not exist, our psychological and spiritual growth would be limited. Our *awareness* of this struggle for realization in our lives influences how we respond to the individual and group differences we perceive. Do such differences enrich our experience of living by underlining the commonality beneath? Do they enrich our experience of living by revealing the commonality underneath? Do they represent a longing for the unrecognized and unacknowledged parts of ourselves that we no longer know? Or, are differences seen as alien symbols that further isolate us not only from others but from ourselves as well?

In many respects, the accident of our birth and the trauma inherent in socialization determine how open we are to ourselves, which in turn influences our acceptance of "others." Our culture influences the direction of the human struggle to become ourselves, but the options that most appeal to us are ultimately a reflection of our relationship with ourselves. Even the way we respond to a truth is telling. In the words of David J. Lieberman, PhD, "A truth that you acknowledge does not offend. Nor does a lie that you know to be false. Only a truth that you don't want to recognize as such causes you pain." 1

Denys has identified some basic disciplines and skills for developing emotional self-mastery and the ability to relate to others effectively. His description of "core disciplines of emotional intelligence" represents a good place to start. Should you experience difficulty in implementing one of these, think of the difficulty as offering potentially valuable information about yourself. Ask yourself questions you think someone very different from you might ask. You need only ask the question and remain open to the possibility there is something to discover about yourself.

The peculiarity exists that one can see in others only that which is in the self. The more unhealthy a person's behavior tends to be, the less differentiated are the responses they receive from others. Healthy, mature individuals live in a differentiated world, where they are constantly offered opportunities to expand their perspectives and to challenge their fixed social constructions regarding themselves. The freedom that others experience to be creative in relationship to us and to express fully who they perceive themselves to be is, in the aggregate, a measure of *our* psychological health and maturity.

William D. Anton, PhD
President and CEO
CEOEffectiveness.com
Tampa, Florida

Disclaimer

Medical Advice

The information, ideas, and suggestions in this book are not intended as a substitute for professional medical advice. Before following any suggestions contained in this book, you should consult your personal physician. Neither the author nor the publisher shall be liable or responsible for any loss or damage allegedly arising as a consequence of your use or application of any information or suggestions in this book.

Psychological Advice

The information, ideas, and suggestions in this book are not intended as a substitute for professional advice. Before following any suggestions contained in this book, you should consult your personal physician or mental health professional. Neither the author nor the publisher shall be liable or responsible for any loss or damage allegedly arising as a consequence of your use or application of any information or suggestions in this book.

Preface

As the twenty-first century progresses, our nation is experiencing tremendous population growth. In addition to sheer numbers, the variety of people who now live, learn, and work in the United States is also expanding. This increase in human diversity is reflected in the workforce. Not only are we experiencing increased diversity, reflected in the number of African Americans, Latinos, Asians, and Native Americans, the number of women in our institutions and organizations is also steadily rising.

Many individuals have multiple racial, religious, or ethnic identities, sometimes categorized as "Other." Beyond these categories, the number of people with disabilities, as well as the number of individuals who are openly gay, lesbian, bisexual, and transgender, have also increased. The number of senior citizens in the workforce is also on the rise. This complex diversity is almost mind-boggling, and we have not even considered the differences in class, function, personality, and temperament that cut across the traditional ways we understand diversity.

We are all part of institutions and organizations that reflect our diverse society. This diversity is also reflected in our beliefs, assumptions, and actions toward one another. To be effective and successful and to feel that we belong within our workplace, we must develop the emotional intelligence to relate and get along with others, particularly those who seem to think, look, and sound different from us. This ability is known as social intelligence.

Many efforts by American organizations during the past two decades have centered on valuing and appreciating diversity and differences. These initiatives were the first steps in our nation's efforts to reposition organizations away from past exclusionary practices toward sincere efforts to achieve diversity in the workforce. It has become clear, however, that organizations must move beyond the emphasis on differences toward commonalities and a new level of understanding and learning that will enable us to build highly effective organizations in an increasingly global community.

Current and future efforts must focus on both difference and commonalty, including the relationship between the two. Before we can truly transform diverse populations into authentic communities of learners and workers, we must move through difference toward commonality.

Diversity enables organizations to understand the challenges and opportunities in many business and service environments. But in order for organizations to develop the capacity to understand and respond effectively, team members must have emotional and social intelligence in order to develop effective relationships that enable them to work collaboratively and successfully toward common organizational goals and objectives.

- It is important to realize that before organizations can begin to recognize and understand differences we must first seek to recognize, understand and value the things and interests we have in common. Unless we start with our commonalties, we will find no reason or motivation to seek an understanding and appreciation of differences. Further, when beginning with commonalties, we lay the groundwork for dialogue when we do deal with differences, rather than problems. Our shared humanity offers the best starting place for finding a common identity that transcends our differences.

Our fundamental commonalties as human beings include:

- The same fundamental psychological, social, and emotional needs. Recognizing this commonalty makes it possible to believe in the worth and dignity of any person, regardless of difference.

- The same fundamental need to be trusted, respected, forgiven, and treated with care and fairness, without prejudice and stereotype, and to have our uniqueness and differences valued and understood.

- Our destinies, survival, and prosperity are interconnected and interdependent. We will either flourish or perish together.

As associates of interconnected organizations, our livelihoods are interdependent. We share interest in each other's success. Indeed, we are likely to share each other's successes and failures.

We have a lot more at stake regarding our common interests than our differences. This means we need to remember that our specific actions at home and at work affect the way our families, teams, and organizations function. Our actions come back to us indirectly as we are shaping our social environment in the form of our organizations, communities, and families. In general, we co-create all our experiences. Therefore, we must take care with what we create. The ability to work effectively and successfully in the diverse organization—to shift beyond diversity to commonalities—requires emotional intelligence.

Finally, commonalties are the foundation of any community. Fundamentally, a community is a system of relationships between people with, first and foremost, common interests. This does not deny difference. Rather, it makes interest in and concerns for difference a common value. Thus, by beginning with commonalty, appreciating and understanding differences becomes a greater priority, one that comes from within a community rather than being imposed on it from outside. This is why it is essential that we must move beyond diversity and differences to commonalities as the foundation of building effective organizations and communities. And for this shift to successfully occur in diverse organizations, emotional intelligence is required. But what is emotional intelligence? [1]

In many ways, this book seeks to address a promise Bob Kreisher and I made in our book, *No Place to Hide in America:* [2] to offer a solution to many of the diversity-related problems we identified in that book. I believe the approaches recommended in this book are antidotes to the behaviors that create many of the problems and challenges associated with building authentic communities in the diverse workplace. While this book offers a prescription for individual behavior, I am currently working on another book that will offer a conceptual and theoretical model for building authentic and emotional intelligent communities within diverse organizations.

Acknowledgements

This book is the result of years of work on the topic of building diverse and authentic communities in a diverse society. My indebtedness extends to my friend and coauthor of many publications, including our book *No Place to Hide in America*, Robert D. Kreisher, who coauthored with me a previous manuscript on the same topic. Although the present work represents more than a mere revision of our original manuscript, his influence on the content and structure remains. Thank you, Bob.

My gratitude also extends to my friend and mentor William Anton, for contributing the forward to this book and for granting permission to use *What is in a Name?* in this book.

I am also grateful to Susan Hall for her willingness to read the manuscript and provide me with significant feedback and suggestions that were helpful in making my ideas clearer and readable.

My appreciation and gratitude also extends to Joseph Young for designing the book cover. Thank you, Joe, for your patience as we worked through the design. Joe can be reached via email at jygraphicd@yahoo.com .

I am also grateful to the many individuals who, over the years, attended my workshops and encouraged me to put my ideas in the form of a book. I have now done that and hope you will like it.

Finally, I would like to acknowledge Alacia Edwards for her assistance with finalizing the manuscript for submission.

Contents

Introduction

One hallmark of emotional intelligence is the capacity for collaboration. This capacity to do things *with* others generates *authentic power*: [1]. the most sustainable type of individual and systemic power in organizations. Authentic power is the result of individual and collective mastery of the core emotional disciplines of authenticity and emotional intelligence, which are unconditional trust, respect, honesty, truth, fairness, openness, care, and forgiveness. These are highly prized virtues in many organizations. Other types of individual and systemic powers—what Blain Lee in *Power Principle* calls *coercive power* [2] (the capacity to do things to others) and *utility power* (the capacity to do things for others)—respectively engender independence and codependence and are not sustainable. [3]

The level of your emotional intelligence or authentic power determines the quality of your interactions and relationships (social intelligence) capacity for collaboration, and success in life and at work. Systemic power (also called authentic power) defined by authentic relationships is generated by emotionally intelligent, authentic, and interdependent individuals who live, learn, and work in the same organization and community. Many of us seek to embody and practice these virtues and disciplines and, with the help of this book and personal development programs, may develop the emotional intelligence essential to building authentic relationships across differences, which are critical to collaboration.

You can't be authentic with others if you are not first authentic with yourself. The ability to embody the core emotional disciplines of authenticity is the result of your capacity to be unconditionally trusting, respectful, fair, truthful, honest, open, caring, and forgiving with yourself. That is why the transformative process involved in developing basic emotional intelligence is called *self-mastery.*[4] Self-mastery is crucial, no matter what position you occupy in your organization.

The emotional brain learns from repetition: practice/learn, practice/learn, practice/learn. As you proceed through this book, take one discipline or related behavior at a time and practice/learn.

Choose to change only one behavior at a time, because that is the way the emotional brain learns and relearns. Make a commitment to stay the course, even when you encounter obstacles and difficulties, and never give up. Keep practicing and learning from the experience until you master the new discipline and accompanying behavior. It is not going to be easy at first, because some behaviors are based on memories that may be very painful or buried deep in the unconscious memory.

With commitment and perseverance (practice, practice, practice), it is possible to master new behaviors and become successful.

Chapter 1

What is Emotional Intelligence?

Emotional intelligence is the ability to understand, discipline, and express emotions (impulse management) and to respond to the emotions of those with whom we live, learn, and work.[1] Emotional intelligence determines our personal patterns of interactions and the quality of the relationships we develop. When we are emotionally intelligent we have the ability to control our emotions, which affect the way we relate to others, the quality of our relationships, and our sustained success in the diverse workplace. Emotional intelligence is embodied by emotional self-mastery. We are emotionally intelligent and authentic when, through self-mastery and impulse management, we learn to embody the disciplines of unconditional trust, respect, honesty, truth, fairness, care, openness, and forgiveness.

What is Social Intelligence?

Emotional intelligence is about the qualities of the individual, while social intelligence [2] is about the qualities (pattern and type) [3] of social interactions between individuals and among people. These qualities determine the type of relationships and the type of power they collectively generate. Social intelligence means individuals in the group have embodied the disciplines of authenticity and are able to relate to others in ways that build and sustain authentic relationships.

Social intelligence is the capacity for relating to others in a manner that builds and sustains authentic relationships and systems. This type of relationship is defined by what Martin Buber calls *"I-Thou"* relationships [4]. In short, this means we treat others as subjects and not as objects to be threatened, manipulated, controlled, and used. Subject-to-subject relationships are the foundation of the golden rule.

What Happened to Us?

It is too often the case in modern American society that child-rearing does not lead to emotionally healthy children. Sometime during a child's upbringing, something or someone (consciously or unconsciously; intentionally or unintentionally) hurts the child or a traumatic event leaves a lasting emotional impression (trauma). The level of severity of this traumatic experience (fear) determines how such children are affected after the event. There are two common types of post traumatic impressions: post-traumatic stress disorder and post traumatic stress syndrome, [5] and they determine the level and type of fear experienced and, over time, how the person feels and behaves. Emotions and moods determine patterns of actions and interactions (behavior).

There is an old folk story about a hiker in the desert who angrily chased a rattlesnake that had bit him. He finally cornered and killed the snake thirty minutes later. By the time he realized he needed medical care for the snake bite, the pain had become unbearable; the poison had traveled through his veins to his vital organs. He went into toxic shock a few hours later and died before he could get any help. Had he focused on dealing with the poison immediately, he might have saved his own life. Instead of dealing with the poison, he chased and killed the snake. [6]

Realize that after any hurtful experience, you always have a choice of either dealing with the poison or emotionally chasing the proverbial snake that "bit" you years ago, watching yourself slowly die emotionally from the poison. Accept that though you may not be responsible for the original trauma, you now have the responsibility for doing something about the poison in order to manage its effect on your life, if you are to live and grow emotionally. The choice is yours; exercise it and discover the exhilarating power of free will and volition. You are the one that has the most to gain from dealing with the poison.

Remember that forgiveness is not something that you do for someone else; it is something that you do for yourself. When you stay angry with someone, you have made that person a part of your life [7]. Unconditionally forgiving yourself and those who have hurt you are very powerful ways of healing the pain and shame caused by the hurts and humiliation experienced long ago when the snake bit you.

What is trauma?

The degree of intensity of a traumatic experience determines which of the two types you develop:

1. Post traumatic stress disorder (PTSD), or
2. Post traumatic stress syndrome (PTSS)

In the first, PTSD, the experience was so intense that you believed you were going to lose your life. In the second, PTSS, the experience was not as intense; you were not seriously hurt, but the experience was demeaning and humiliating. The psychological symptoms of the two are the same, except for the degree of intensity. While intensity differentiates PTSD from PTSS, the symptoms are generally the same. They include fear, anxiety, chronic insomnia, guilt, explosive temper, depression, eating disorders, difficulty focusing, substance abuse, and relationship problems. 8

In both cases, trauma affects breathing, starves the brain of oxygen, and over time determines your mood and how you feel and behave. Walking long distances, as described below, is critical to changing how you breathe. In some cases, however, walking alone may not be sufficient. You may need to seek the help of a professional therapist.

How does trauma affect us over time?

A traumatic experience affects your breathing and how you feel. The amygdala, the part of the emotional brain that is the human alarm system responsible for protecting you from danger, is very intensely aroused. This experience causes your breathing to automatically switch from deep abdominal breathing to frequent but shallow chest breathing, helping your heart pump Adrenaline saturates blood flowing to the large muscles. Adrenaline gives you the energy and strength to fight for your survival or to run like hell away from danger and possible death, to save your life. [9]

Chronic high-level arousal of the amygdala leaves it permanently aroused, requiring medication to calm it down so that you are not relieving the traumatic experience over and over again after the event. Medication, psychotherapy, and regular exercise help you maintain relative emotional calmness. Without treatment, the arousal of the amygdala means you generate too much energy in your large muscles, caused by excess adrenaline in the blood stream, for the task in which you are involved. Too much energy in the large muscles causes stress and eventually, over time, can lead to hypertension, or high blood pressure, and other problems.

This is also true in situations in which the experience was sub-traumatic and not as severe as the former. Repeated arousal of the amygdala beyond the normal range over time also affects its ability to return to its original level of calmness. Though not as extreme as PTSD, PTSS nonetheless leaves the amygdala aroused beyond its normal range, generating too much energy in the large muscles for the task at hand. One of the most common effects of PTSS is generalized anxiety. The continually aroused amygdala manifests as stress. We know that when you are already emotionally stressed you will overact to everything that happens around you. This is why it's sometimes said that stress makes people stupid.

Remember that the arousal of amygdala automatically switches your breathing from deep abdominal breathing to frequent but shallow chest breathing to help the heart pump blood and adrenaline to the large muscles. Shallow chest breathing constricts the flow of oxygen to the blood vessels to allow adrenaline to work. This means that you are receiving only the bare minimum of oxygen required to stay alive. To reverse this, you must interrupt your breathing by switching to deep abdominal, or diaphragmatic, breathing. To sustain deep breathing, teach yourself how to unconsciously breathe deeply from the abdomen out. One way to do this is through long distance walking.

If you continually experience stress, you may want to consider seeking professional help to determine the sources of the stress in your life and to find out if medication may help reduce the anxiety that is manifesting as stress. Medications such as Zoloft or

Zanax are often very effective in reducing the level of anxiety. When supplemented by regular exercise or meditation, the combination may transform how you feel and behave, as well as the quality of your work. Please consult your medical or mental health doctor for proper evaluation to determine if medication is appropriate for you.

How Does Deep Diaphragmatic, Abdominal Breathing Help with Impulse Management?

Regular exercise and deep abdominal breathing release beta endorphins, especially oxytocin and serotonin, into the bloodstream. Oxytocin and serotonin are hormonal endorphins that enhance the body's ability to transport oxygen to the emotional brain and have an immediate calming effect on the amygdala to reduce anxiety. The more you exercise and breathe deeply, the more oxytocin and serotonin you will produce and the calmer you will become. The calmer you become, the greater your ability to manage reactive emotional impulses. Remember that deep breathing achieved through regular exercise, meditation, yoga, or other means is critical to impulse management and emotional intelligence. [10]

How does one learn to embody deep breathing for emotional calmness?

An essential part of the process of developing basic emotional intelligence is a commitment to regular exercise and deep breathing. While exercise in general, without or without meditation, is good for stress reduction, walking meditation is indispensable to the processes of self-mastery and impulse management. Try the following:

- Check with your personal physician to ensure that your health permits regular walking exercises.
- Begin walking slowly and increase your speed in increments until you reach a comfortable speed.
- Start with a mile a day (morning or evening), and slowly increase your mileage to two miles a day.
- Slowly increase your weekend mileage to three miles each on Saturday and Sunday; continue to increase your mileage by increments of a mile each week until you reach a comfortable mileage.
- Ideally, you should walk a minimum of between fifteen and twenty miles a week to get the full benefit.

Use this quiet time to reflect on your strengths and on areas of potential growth with regards to the core emotional disciplines, the changes that you would like to make, and what the eventual outcomes would mean for you. You may reflect on the "Emotional Intelligence Profile" in the appendix of this book, particularly the feedback you received from a friend, colleague, or coworker who has worked with you and knows you very well. Consider one discipline at a time, and remember that the emotional brain learns in deep cycles of practicing and learning repeated over and over again. It is not going to be easy at first; some memories of trauma are very painful, buried deep in the emotional brain, commonly called the unconscious mind.

Remember: the process of self-mastery begins with *self-awareness*. Consider the feedback you receive from a colleague or coworker as the beginning point of the process of emotional self-mastery. The next step is for you to reflect on the source(s) or cause(s) of the problem of which you are now aware. This part of the process, *self-examination*, is essential to self-understanding. At this point, you are not only aware of the behaviors that need to change; you have also examined them and are now in the process of understanding how and why the problems exist. At this stage in the process, you are well on your way to the next step: *self-understanding*. Continually paying attention to how you feel during the course of the day will provide you with opportunities to examine those feelings that will help you develop self-understanding. When you understand yourself, you are more likely to become more motivated to do something about it. *Self-understanding* is the motivation and energy source for *self-motivation*, which enables you to control or manage the specific emotional impulses that are creating the undesired feelings, behaviors, and problems. In turn, self-understanding is the source behind the motivation and energy essential to *self-discipline* and *self-mastery*.

If you discover something too painful, traumatic, or difficult to deal with, please seek the professional assistance of a clinical psychologist or psychotherapist. Do not try to deal with it alone.

As you continue in this process, you will slowly begin to experience changes in the way you feel and behave. Most importantly, you will begin to exercise more control over the emotional impulses that prompt you to *react* to the things that are happening around you, allowing you to *respond* appropriately, what Steven Covey calls *response-ability* [11]. The more impulse management you are able to exercise, the more EI capability you will experience. Good luck!

What Are the Benefits of Emotional Intelligence?

The benefits of emotional intelligence are success and satisfaction in your professional as well as personal lives. Your capacity for success is directly tied to your level of emotional intelligence. Improving your emotional intelligence will lead to reduced fear and anxiety about relationships with people, particularly those who are different from you. This comes about not because you are confident that you will always know what to say but because over time you have developed strong relationships, and you know how to continue developing these relationships for the long-term. New relationships will become less stressful and easier to develop with the more practice and success you experience. When you have strong relationships with those who live, work, and learn with you, it shows in your attitude and the attitude of others toward you.

These attitudes become self-fulfilling prophecies. When people perceive this attitude, they expect that you will be trustworthy and likeable. And we usually see what we expect to see. When we are emotionally intelligent, we tend to develop relationships that lead to personal satisfaction, happiness, and professional success.

What Are the Dimensions of EI in an Authentic and Diverse Organization?

There are three dimensions of emotional intelligence in the authentic and diverse organization. They are:
- Impulse management
- Self-mastery
- Authenticity

What is Impulse Management?

Impulse management is the ability to manage the emotional impulses that prompt us to react in difficult and potential conflict situations. Impulse management is the key to our ability to be responsive instead of reactive and is critical to slowing down the speed and need to become judgmental about the people and the difficult issues with which we struggle. It is essential to our emotional intelligence but also critical to our level of cognitive intelligence. The ability to understand and listen to what others are saying is enhanced by slowing down the need to become argumentative and disagreeable.

Impulse management also requires the will to accept the need for change, the resolve to practice the new disciplines, and the commitment to learn from mistakes and shortfalls as we master the new disciplines.

How Does One Develop Emotional Intelligence?

Some people are born with emotional intelligence. It is a gift. For this, they are admired and respected. But most of us have to learn new ways of relating to others that enable us to communicate better and build stronger relationships. Those of us who do not have the "natural talent" to relate well to everyone have a choice about whether or not to learn to emotionally discipline ourselves. Because change is inevitable, you may wish to change in ways that you desire instead of leaving it up to chance and the will of other people.

Being open to change is the first step in the process of developing emotional intelligence. There is nothing more rewarding than exercising your free will to change. Indeed, it is much more satisfying than waiting around to change according to chance, your environment, or your boss. Our level of emotional intelligence is measured by our capacity for self-renewal and ability to have satisfying relationships at work and elsewhere. The capacity for self-renewal is essential for continual change, growth, and sustained success in a diverse and dynamic society.

As I said earlier, the beginning of the process of self-transformation is the acceptance of the need for change and the will to do so. This is not easy because many of us are in denial about the need to change. It takes courage to realize and admit that our life needs to take a turn for the better. Some of us wait until we are forced to change. Once you have truly accepted the need to change, you need to determine as clearly as possible what change will look like after it is embodied—in other words, having a clear vision of what you want to achieve and what new behaviors you would like to embody look like. The more clearly you can visualize the change, the more power you will have to practice and learn the new behaviors. Change requires the perseverance and self-discipline described in the section on self-mastery. Beyond visualization, you will need the emotional resolve and persistence to succeed.

The degree of success you will experience in the diverse workplace will reflect your emotional and social intelligence, which is a function of the degree to which you emotionally master the core disciplines of trust, respect, honesty, truth, fairness, care, openness, and forgiveness.

The vision will not be clear at first. Clarifying the vision is a continual process that takes practice as you learn the new emotional disciplines. It occurs in a cycle of practicing and learning [12] from the experience and trying over and over again until you are successful. In other words, you will have to *fake it 'til you make it.*[13] The new behavior becomes hard-wired after eighteen to twenty consecutive successful practices of the new behavior. You will also need to start over again when there is a slip until the new behavior is embodied.

Developing basic EI requires *commitment* to:
- Personal and shared visions
- New emotional disciplines (values of authenticity)
- Emotional self-mastery and deep learning
- Impulse management

In certain cases, professional assistance is necessary. The process also requires meditation and deep breathing exercises or long distance walking meditation (see *How Does One Learn to Embody Deep Breathing for Emotional Calmness?* on page 26.

What is Commitment?

The impetus for commitment to some course of action comes from within a person. Commitment is the result of personal and shared aspirations and cannot be mandated or forced. One characteristic difference from compliance is the practice of personal accountability in commitment. For when we are in a compliance mode, we tend to blame something or someone when we encounter difficulties and fail to achieve mandated performance goals. [14]

What is Emotional Self-Mastery?

Emotional self-mastery is a six-step process of deep learning of the new emotional disciplines and behaviors essential to achieving authenticity in the diverse workplace. The process of self-mastery involves six sequential steps:

- Self-awareness
- Self-examination
- Self-understanding
- Self-motivation
- Self-discipline
- Self-mastery

Each step in the process represents a prerequisite to the next (see illustration on Emotional Self-mastery and Cycles of Deep Learning on page 35).

How do you achieve self-mastery?

As you saw in the preceding list, emotional self-mastery is a six-step process involving deep learning of the emotional disciplines essential to emotional intelligence and authenticity.

Deep learning results from the commitment to practice new emotional disciplines and behaviors, as well as the willingness to learn from the experience (practice/learn). It is through this process that new behaviors are learned. It can take between twelve and eighteen successful consecutive practices of the new discipline to hard-wire the new behavior. The emotional brain learns and relearns for repeated practice.

The process of self-mastery begins with self-awareness. Start with any feedback regarding your ability to unconditionally trust before any of the other emotional disciplines mentioned above, that you may have received from a supervisor, colleague, or coworker. This is because unconditional trust is the first discipline of emotional intelligence.

The next step is to reflect on the causes of the behavior of which you are now aware and would like to change. This part of the process, self-examination, is essential to the next step of self-understanding. At this point, you are not only aware of the behavior that needs to change but you have examined it and are now in the process of understanding the causes or sources of the behavior. At this stage in the process, you are well on your way to the next step, self-motivation, of managing the emotional impulses that create the feelings, behaviors, and problems. The source of the motivation and energy essential for self-discipline and self-mastery is self-understanding

If you discover something too painful, traumatic, or difficult to deal with during this process, please seek professional assistance from a clinical psychologist or psychotherapist. Don't try to deal with it alone. As you persist and continue in this process, you will slowly begin to experience changes in the way you feel and behave.

The process of emotional self-mastery involves six sequential steps. Each step in the process represents a prerequisite to the next.

Steps to Emotional Self-Mastery

The emotional brain learns in cycles of deep learning that involves practicing new behaviors and learning from the experience until the new disciplines has been mastered.

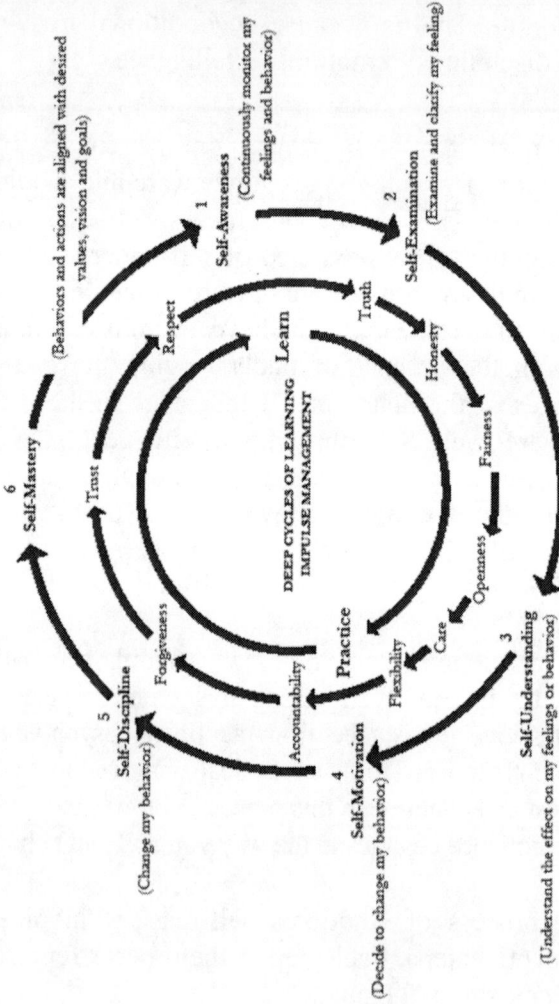

1 Self-Awareness
(Continuously monitor my feelings and behavior)

(Behaviors and actions are aligned with desired values, vision and goals)

2 Self-Examination
(Examine and clarify my feeling)

Respect

Truth

Learn

Honesty

Self-Mastery

Trust

DEEP CYCLES OF LEARNING
IMPULSE MANAGEMENT

Fairness

6

Openness

Care

3 Self-Understanding
(Understand the effect on my feelings or behavior)

Forgiveness

Practice

Flexibility

5 Self-Discipline
(Change my behavior)

Accountability

4 Self-Motivation
(Decide to change my behavior)

Figure One

36

Step One: Self-awareness

Begin by continuously monitoring your feelings and behavior by asking yourself:

- How am I doing, and how am I feeling?
- What feedback have I received recently that will help me with self- awareness?
- What behavior do I need to change to improve my performance and effectiveness?

Step Two: Self-examination

Examine and clarify your feelings by asking yourself:

- Why am I having these feelings?
- Have I had these feelings before?
- When? Where? What happened? What were my feelings at the time?

Step Three: Self-understanding

Understand the effect of your feelings and behavior by asking yourself:

- What are these feelings really about?
- What will happen if I continue to let these feelings determine my behavior?
- How are they affecting my behavior, relationships, and performance?

Step Four: Self-motivation

Decide whether or not to change the behavior by answering the following questions:

- What will happen to benefit me if I change the behavior?
- How can I manage these feelings and my behavior?

Step Five: Self-discipline
Change the behavior by forgiving the past and committing to practicing the new behavior.

- As you remember painful thoughts from the past, forgive yourself and others who caused you pain and embarrassment.
- Commit to beginning to manage your feelings (impulse management), actions, thoughts, and behavior in accordance with the desired disciplines, values, and vision

Step Six: Self-mastery
Your behavior and actions are aligned with desired values, visions, and goals.

- I have forgiven myself and others for the painful events of the past and am ready to move forward (see chapter on forgiveness).
- I can manage my feelings and behavior, and, as a result, I can trust unconditionally again.
- I am aligned emotionally, cognitively, and physically with the desired personal and organizational vision, values, and goals.

The first discipline of emotional intelligence is the capacity to unconditionally trust yourself and others. Failure to master this discipline makes it difficult, if not impossible, to master or practice the other disciplines. Since the first discipline of emotional intelligence and authenticity is unconditional trust, the process of self-mastery must begin with your capacity to trust. How do you develop the capacity for unconditional trust?

What Emotional Disciplines Are Essential to Authenticity In the Diverse Workplace?

The specific disciplines essential to creating emotionally intelligent, authentic, and diverse workplaces, characterized by a satisfying work environment and strong networks of personal relationships, are discussed below. When you have mastered and embodied these disciplines, you will become an emotionally intelligent and authentic change agent for the emergence of a community defined by authentic pluralism, as defined in the next section:

1. Trusting and forgiving unconditionally
2. Recognizing similarities and valuing commonalities
3. Recognizing and understanding differences
4. Dealing with personal prejudice
5. Building relationships across differences
6. Managing differences before they become conflict
7. Doing your best to keep all commitments
8. Practicing personal accountability
9. Being fair with yourself and others
10. Listening carefully for understanding
11. Giving and receive feedback with care
12. Being flexible and open to new ideas
13. Being your best at what you do

Begin by completing the Basic Emotional Intelligence Quiz in Appendix 1 to get a general sense of how emotionally intelligent you are, and then reflect on your responses and total score. To get more specific feedback, consider using the Basic Emotional Intelligence Profile on Appendix 2.

What is Authentic Pluralism?

Authentic pluralism refers to a diverse, integrated, interconnected, and emotionally disciplined community of individuals with deep commitment to a shared vision, core set of values, and collaboration. It is a community in which differences are understood and commonalities serve as the foundation of community. Its members strive to embody the emotional disciplines essential to personal, relational, and systemic authenticity: unconditional trust, respect, openness, honesty, truth, fairness, forgiveness, and care. Members of such a community are emotionally intelligent because they value, embody, and practice self-mastery and impulse management, essential to co-creating and sustaining a shared authentic pluralist community.

Chapter 2

Trust and Forgive Unconditionally

Everyone, like you, will make mistakes. Learning to forgive yourself when you make mistakes is critical to your ability to forgive and trust others. Self-forgiveness is the hardest part. When you find yourself having difficulty forgiving others, it may be because you have not yet forgiven yourself or are finding it difficult to do so. So practice self-forgiveness and develop the ability to forgive others. The easier it becomes to forgive yourself, the easier it will become for you to forgive others.

Be assertive and say what is bothering you. Do not become aggressive and take advantage of the mistakes and errors of others. By being assertive and

> ℰℴℭℛ
>
> *Self-Forgiveness*
>
> *You must forgive yourself unconditionally. Forgiveness is not something you do for someone else, its something you do for yourself—because when you stay angry with someone you make that person a part of your life.*
>
> *- Garrison Kellior*
>
> ℰℴℭℛ

expressing your feelings and by being open to what others have to say about their concerns, you will be seen as a fair person. [1] Always apologize and ask others for forgiveness if you have been unfair or have hurt them (which is one way of being accountable). And always unconditionally forgive those who have hurt and offended you, without demanding an apology.

Let go of anger and do not hold on to grudges, resentments, and prejudices. Remember that your capacity to trust relates directly to your ability to forgive. Each promotes the other, so each little step yields immeasurable results.

In fact, your ability to learn from your mistakes directly relates to your ability to recognizing and admitting your mistakes and forgiving yourself. If you are not willing to admit your mistakes to yourself and forgive yourself for them, you will not grow, and you cannot be effective interpersonally. You will be stuck in your current patterns for the rest of your life.

Why Forgive and Trust Unconditionally?

Forgiving and trusting unconditionally means forgiving yourself and forgiving others for their mistakes and errors. Remember that your capacity to trust directly relates to your capacity to forgive. More specifically, always remember to:

- **Forgive yourself unconditionally.** Most learning takes place through making mistakes and having the courage to recognize and admit them, to yourself at the very least. If you are unwilling to admit your mistakes to yourselves and forgive yourself for them, you will not be able to forgive others;

- **Forgive others unconditionally.** Forgive those who have hurt and offended you without demanding an apology. You must let go of anger and hold no grudges, resentments, or prejudices.
- **Apologize unconditionally.** Apologize and ask for forgiveness if you have been unfair or have hurt others. In fact, the sooner you apologize, the sooner the healing begins and, research has revealed, the easier it becomes to forgive.

Dimensions of Forgiveness

Studies have shown that people who have learned to forgive are indeed happier and healthier than those who hold on to grudges and resentments. Those who are less forgiving reportedly suffer from a variety of illnesses, including nervous system problems, and tend to have greater levels of social and interpersonal relationship problems. Research has also found that learning to forgive oneself and others is not only good for you physically, it is critical to your mental health. 2

There are four types and levels of forgiveness. 3 There are the things we:

- Forgive and never forget
- Never forgive and never forget
- Never forgive but forget
- Forgive and forget

43

What happens when you forgive and never forget?

The next best situation to be in with regard to forgiveness is to forgive while still remembering events of the past, minus the hurtful feelings associated with the memory. When this happens, it means that you have learned from the experience and have forgiven yourself and others as you moved on with your life. You have not forgotten, but you have forgiven. This is why we can sometimes talk and laugh about the once hurtful things that happened in the past. Forgetting is not a prerequisite for forgiveness. The key is to remember the past without the original pain. When you can forgive and still remember without the original pain associated with the memory, you will be able to practice and embody the disciplines of authenticity and become more emotionally intelligent. 4

What happens when you never forgive and never forget?

When you never forgive and never forget past hurts, you will always be in a self-protective mode. You may always be ready for revenge or be waiting for an opportune time to get even. In this revenge or self-protection mode, you will consciously or unconsciously seek revenge and hurt others. You are probably perceived as mean-spirited or, in extreme cases, evil, because people find it difficult to accept that you can consciously seek to hurt others, even those who have not hurt you in the past. Moffitt tells us:

"Tragically, you become one with anger; you are now its servant. It is a reactive rather than a proactive manner of living, one that is based on doing to another, not on being with your self. It implies a false promise of peace: *If only you could make them pay.* There are many examples of this resentment becoming a person's identity to the degree that he is made grandiose by it, thinking he uniquely knows the will of God to punish and is therefore supposed to act on it." [5]

What happens when you never forgive but forget?

What happens when you never forgive but forget about the things that happened and those who hurt you in the distant past?

This is the source of most of the unconscious impulses that drive negative behaviors and adversely affect our interactions and relationships. It is commonly accepted among psychoanalysts that traumatic memory buried deep in the unconscious memory generates the strongest impulses that drive our feelings and behavior. The deeper the un-forgiven pain is buried, the greater the chance that even though you have forgotten, you have not forgiven. In tis case, you have to become intentional and practice the disciplines of self-mastery, starting with self-awareness and self-examination, to begin the journey

45

toward self-understanding and self-forgiveness. In some cases, you may need the professional assistance of a therapist to safely go deep enough to begin the process of healing the hurts that are driving your feelings and behavior.

What happens when you forgive and forget?

Perhaps the best possible thing is to forgive and forget. When you forgive and forget the pains of the past, you tend to hold no grudges and have no need for revenge and, therefore, can be accepting of others. When you hold no grudges and have no need for revenge or to protect yourself, you can be free to practice and embody the disciplines of authenticity. You will be able to become unconditionally trusting, respectful, fair, honest, truthful, open, and caring in your interactions with others. When you are able to do this, you become more emotionally intelligent than you would have had you not forgotten and forgiven.

Can We Learn to Forgive?

Some experts in Eastern religions and philosophies teach forgiveness through meditation and other means. No matter what method you use, forgiveness is perhaps one of the most difficult things to achieve, especially if you have suffered the loss of a loved one or if you or someone you really care about was treated unfairly, cruelly, or violently. Maybe it was a crime of hate, sexual violence, incest, or spousal cheating or betrayal—no matter how great or small the offence, the experience left you bitter and unable to trust again. The experience has now left you with a sense of entitlement for revenge. But as Phillip Moffitt tells us:

"There is no entitlement for revenge, no right to hate, and no right to think your grief, loss, and confusion are unique or entitle you to torture another ... to meet hatred and loss with love and a generous heart is the most difficult practice imaginable. Sometimes I hesitate to teach it, for I have my own struggles with anger and hardening of the heart as a reaction to terrible and unjust acts. Yet what is the purpose of a practice if you are not going to use it in life's difficult moments? It requires humility to surrender to the mystery of life, its unpredictability. It requires an equal amount of courage to face life's losses and be willing to say, *'This too is life'* and bear it as you find it, even while doing everything in your power to change it into a gentler, safer experience." 6

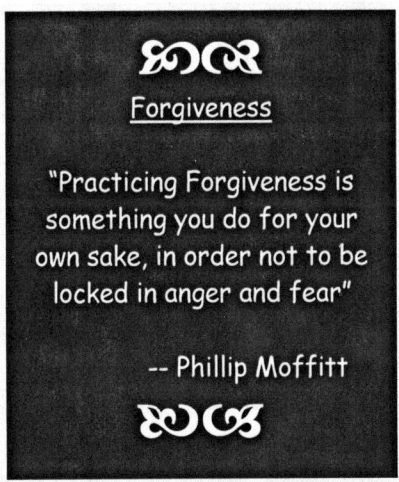

> ଚ୍ଚ ଔଷ
> <u>Forgiveness</u>
>
> "Practicing Forgiveness is something you do for your own sake, in order not to be locked in anger and fear"
>
> -- Phillip Moffitt
> ଚ୍ଚ ଔଷ

How Does Forgiveness Work?

Human beings are fully capable of forgiveness, but it takes discipline and practice. The process goes hand in hand with the process of self-mastery described in chapter one. The beginning point is to ask for forgiveness from all those who may have been harmed because of something that you said or did. This may require a direct apology to those who are still around and are accessible. Then you must ask for forgiveness from those who are gone and cannot be reached or are deceased and accepting their forgiveness in absentia. Finally, forgive yourself for any embarrassment or harm you may have caused yourself over the years. 7

The most critical part of this process involves forgiving yourself and others every time you remember something painful. This means reminding yourself every time you remember something painful that you have already forgiven. Keep doing this every time you feel the pain, and slowly you will find the pain lessening. Every time you remember pain associated with a memory from the past, remind yourself that you have forgiven; the pain will not be as strong the next time you remember, until eventually, with persistence, you can remember the events with very little of the pain associated with the memory. When you can remember what happened with very little associated pain, you will have forgiven.

If you find it difficult to forgive yourself and others, please seek professional assistance to get help with the feelings, because unresolved pain from the past has profound effects on you mentally, professionally, and physically.

Why Is the Ability to Trust a Function of Emotional Discipline?

Trust is not a skill. It is an essential emotional discipline. Trusting one's self is a precondition for learning, embodying, and practicing all of the other core disciplines and behaviors that define an emotionally intelligent and authentic person and community.

How does one develop the capacity to trust unconditionally?

The capacity to trust yourself and others unconditionally is exercised through impulse management and suspending immediate judgment until you have sufficient information and, indeed, the need to make a judgment. This ability to remain open without immediate judgment is critical to the individual and collective capability to co-create a culture of trust that empowers collaboration in your organization. The emotional capacity to be unconditionally open to others and what they have to say and offer is essential to one's capacity to trust others.

You are invited to embark on or recommit to the life-long journey of learning to embody the first discipline of emotional intelligence and authenticity: the capacity to trust unconditionally.

What Is Trust?

Trust is essentially about the unknown. It is the key to

the quality of human relationships and organizational dynamics. Trust is one of the deepest human emotions, as is fear. Trust between a group of people can permeate and determine the quality of everything they do interpersonally and collectively. At its core, trust is deeply interpersonal; when it exists between a group of people, it is said to exponentially improve their collective intelligence and capability. Its absence can make achieving anything meaningful interpersonally or organizationally difficult to impossible. Some social scientists have argued that trust become a critical necessity in high-risk situations and during times of uncertainty. There are basically four levels of trust.8

What Are the Four Levels of Trust?
In general, there are four major types of trust:

1. Mistrust
2. Distrust
3. Conditional trust(negotiated and cooperative)
4. Unconditional trust 9

What Is Mistrust?
Mistrust is not as strong an emotion as distrust and is usually associated with one's self. Mistrust exists when there is some doubt about the outcome of a future event. When it exists in relation to others, it is usually associated with feelings of apprehension and slight uncertainty about the character of another person or their behavior in respect to the outcome of a

future event: *I am not sure he will not backstab me again in the future.* Mistrust can also apply to doubt regarding one's self. It is much easier to transition from mistrust to trust than distrust to trust. [10]

What Is Distrust?

Distrust is a stronger and more emphatic emotion born out of outright suspicion and a complete absence of trust, usually associated with others. Unlike the mistrust—for instance, *I am not sure he will not steal from her again*—distrust would likely be phrased as *I am certain he will steal from her again because he has done so in the past.* [11] Distrust is usually characterized by the expression *Trust but verify* and goes to the heart of distrust. The need to verify suggests the absence of trust. With mistrust, you may give others the benefit of the doubt without the need for verification; with distrust, you give no benefit of the doubt and, therefore, must verify to be reassured. Distrust is the opposite end of conditional trust.

Distrust suggests trust has been broken before. People tend to distrust because of previous experiences with a given person or group or circumstance.

What Is Conditional Trust?

Conditional trust is earned trust, requiring advance proof or evidence of trustworthiness before trust can be given or bestowed (a *prove to me that you are deserving of my trust* kind of mentality) and may, under the right circumstance, become a stepping stone to unconditional trust. [12] Try it if you are having problems with unconditional trust. Some individuals may choose this as a stepping stone to unconditional trust. If, for one reason or another, you choose to take a developmental approach to embodying the ability to trust unconditionally, that is fine, as long as this step is transitory and does not become a permanent utility stage defined by *quid pro quos.*

There are two kinds of conditional trust: *negotiated* and *cooperative* trust. Both of these can eventually lead to unconditional trust, depending on your willingness and commitment to learn and grow and whether or not the environment is supportive.

Negotiated trust entails abiding by negotiated agreements that ensure compliance and set clear expectations for each person involved in the enterprise (*I will do only what is expected, and you will do the same).* These can be legally binding agreements. The hope is that the ability to trust unconditionally will eventually evolve from this stage, to the point where an agreement is no longer necessary to trust unconditionally. [13]

Cooperative trust involves following a step-by-step prescribed process (*I do this, and you do that).*

While unconditional trust is the most sustainable, you may choose one of the two types of conditional trust just discussed that is appropriate for you as you start on the path to self-mastery. You will find yourself progressing to the next level until slowly you discover you are beginning to trust unconditionally.

Remember that your ability to forgive unconditionally directly determines your ability to trust others unconditionally. Try practicing both disciplines (trusting and forgiving) at the same time. This will make the journey much easier. If you find yourself stuck, try asking yourself the following questions; remain open for the response to reveal itself. Ask yourself:

- *What has happened in my past that is affecting my ability to trust now?*
- *What happened in my past that has sapped my ability to trust ever again?*
- *Have my past experiences sapped my ability to trust ever again?*

What Is Unconditional Trust?

Unconditional trust is not earned; it is given, granted, or bestowed upon another person. [14] It does not require advance proof or evidence of trustworthiness. Unconditional trust is the ability to remain open in your interactions, without judgment about others and what they have to say or contribute. It is the result of mastery over the emotional impulses that impel us to be judgmental before we have sufficient information. Trust means you are confident in your expectations that others mean well and are committed to doing no harm. Trusting in the motives and intensions of others without affirmative information and expectations of proof or evidence thereof is unconditional trust. If you practice impulse management consistently, you will learn to trust unconditionally.

Chapter 3

Recognize Similarities and Value Commonalties

As you strive to recognize and understand the visible and invisible elements inherent in the diversity of humanity in your workplace and society, you should also learn to recognize, understand, and value those things that you have in common with others in your community and workplace. Your shared humanity offers the best starting point for finding a common identity to transcend differences. Recognizing commonality makes it possible to believe in and respect the worth and dignity in another person, regardless of differences.

> ଐଓଅ
> ## Commonalties
> Remember that our commonalties give meaning and purpose to our differences. For if it were not for our common interests, there would be no need to manage our differences.
> -Denys Blell& Rober Kreisher (1998)
> ଐଓଅ

When you respect the worth and dignity of others, conflicts and misunderstandings do not disappear. Nonetheless, they do become easier to deal with,

54

because you are more likely to behave in patterns that resolve rather than intensify them.

As residents of the same nation working and living together within the same community and organizations, we have many more common interests than we usually recognize. As people, our destinies, survival, and prosperity are interconnected and interdependent. We will either perish or flourish together. This applies even to a small group, such as your team, your department, your organization, or your circle of friends. When you remember that your specific actions in these groups affect the way the group functions in general, you can acknowledge that you will truly perish or flourish together.

What Do We Mean By Commonalities?

As human beings we have the same fundamental needs. Recognizing this commonality makes it possible to believe in the worth and dignity in every person, regardless of differences. Here are the most fundamental of our commonalities:

- As people, our destinies, survival, and prosperity are interconnected and interdependent. We will either flourish or perish together.
- As citizens of the same nation and residents of the same state, working and living in the same community, we have a lot of common interests.
- As associates of the same organization, our

livelihoods are also interconnected and interdependent.

- As members of the same team, we have a lot of common interest in our collective effectiveness and success.

How are we similar?

We must recognize that, as human beings, we all have the same potential for tremendous good and, paradoxically, the same potential for tremendous evil. Likewise, we share the same choices between the two.

This is why we must all commit ourselves to emotional impulse management and self-mastery and exercise the choice to be a force of good in our organization and society. This means we must understand that the secret to managing our differences lies in our similarities as human beings. [1]

Chapter 4

Recognize and Understand Differences

Diversity refers to the variety of human differences, experiences, belief systems, and perspectives present in our society.

Be open to differences; do not ignore them. Recognize and understand different perspectives, ideas, and opinions because they can only enrich your understanding of people, problems, and issues. In conversations, leave room for different ideas and opinions that others may have— not just to be nice but because you will also benefit.

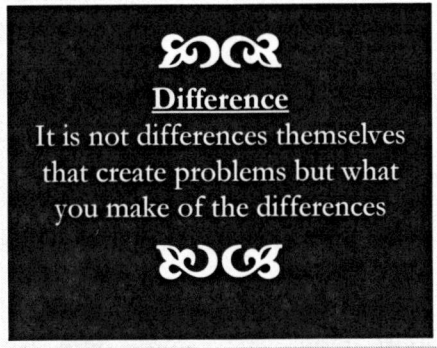

ℰℭ

Difference

It is not differences themselves that create problems but what you make of the differences

ℰℭ

Complexity is the source of intelligence and creativity. So being open is not about accepting everything.

Ultimately, you will be more intelligent and creative if you can learn to slow down your process for coming to conclusions and judgments. In short, let meaning develop more slowly, rather than letting emotions spur you to judgment. Those who assume they do not know are actually perceived as being more intelligent by others than those who assume they do know.

Those who believe they do know, even if they sometimes seem to be right, come off as arrogant, opinionated, and unapproachable. Recognize differences in human variety in your communities and places of work and learning. Learn more about the various cultures present. Openly celebrate them; do not ignore them, because variety enriches our lives and experiences. Seek to develop friendships with others who seem different from you. Connect and get along across differences at the interpersonal level to create a network of relationships that will support your and the organization's success.

What Do We Mean By Recognizing and Understanding Differences?

In spite of what you may have heard about being color blind, do observe and recognize differences in the human variety and experiences in your community and place of work. This means learning more about the people you work with and their cultures and being open about your background and willing to share information about your culture.

The trick is to recognize difference without immediate judgment. Recognize and remain open to different ideas, perspectives, and opinions because they can enrich your understanding of people, issues, and problems.

Also be flexible about the perceptions and practices in your culture that need to change. All cultures have elements that may need to change, particularly when they are conflict with and violate the shared values and vision of your organization and community. Be open to conversations and questions about anything regarding your culture that others find offensive and problematic. Do not become defensive and behave as if your culture is sacred. No culture is sacred or without problems. Cultures that do not change and evolve are moribund. And remember that culture is a reflection of the emotional development of a people. This means that there is always room for change and growth in every culture.

Living and working within an organization and community requires adjusting and changing various cultural attitudes and behaviors. Sometimes the most dysfunctional behaviors and cultural elements are the most resistant to change. We know that the feeling of belonging and mattering in a community or organization occurs when you give up something or exchange a particular behavior for a better or healthier organization and community. [1] If you are not willing to do this, then you will not feel a sense of belonging. You will always feel like an outsider on the margins if you refuse to change those behaviors that the organization or community finds unacceptable. Do not wait until others force you to change; do so with your own free will, and experience what it truly means to be one with your community or organization. Most importantly, when you adapt of your own free will and volition, you will be the primary beneficiary.

Similarly, do not hesitate to question and challenge the behaviors of other that you find offensive and in violation of the stated values and vision of your organization and community. Be polite and curious at first, and then state your views about the behavior as it relates to the shared values and vision. Be careful to ensure that you yourself are not guilty of the same behavior. As Steven Covey tells us, *"Seek first to understand and then be understood."* [2]

In addition, ensure that if you are going to question and challenge the behaviors and cultures of others that you are also open to having your culture and behavior questioned and challenged by others.

What Makes People Different?

As George Simon tells us in *Working Together*, people are different in three fundamental ways:
1. Biology
2. Culture
3. Personality

He argues: *"Most biological differences do not mean much in themselves. It's what you make of the difference that really matters. This means that you need to pay more attention to the second and third factors of culture and personality. Ultimately, however, it's what certain personalities make of biological as well as cultural differences, not the differences themselves, that create problems of intolerance, discrimination, and prejudice in human behavior."* [3]

Why Is Diversity Important?

The challenges and opportunities that our organizations face are the results of the diversity and complexity of the society we serve. In order to respond effectively to those challenges, not only must our organization become as diverse in composition as the society we serve, but we must transform ourselves to achieve greater levels of internal complexity than the perceived complexity of the society we serve, in order to develop the individual and collective capacity to understand and effectively respond to those challenges and opportunities. [4]

However, the qualities of the relationships between the people in your organization will determine the relationship system you co-create, your capacity for collaboration, and your collective intelligence and potential for creativity and innovation. Emotional and social intelligence determine the quality of the relationships and type of power you collectively generate.

Diversity, Creativity and Innovation

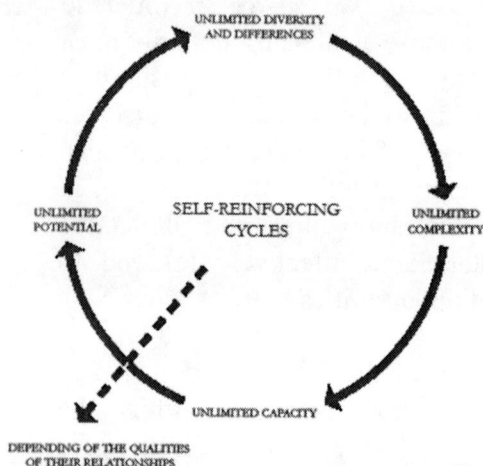

UNLIMITED DIVERSITY
AND DIFFERENCES

SELF-REINFORCING
CYCLES

UNLIMITED
POTENTIAL

UNLIMITED
COMPLEXITY

UNLIMITED CAPACITY

DEPENDING OF THE QUALITIES
OF THEIR RELATIONSHIPS

The challenges and opportunities that organizations face are created by the diversity and complexity of the society they serve. For organizations to respond effectively to those challenges, they must become diverse in their composition, in order to create a greater level of internal complexity that is essential to developing the capacity for understanding the challenges and opportunities.

The type and level of trust in the interactions and behaviors of people who live and work together, determine the qualities of their relationships, the social system that emerges, their collective intelligence to understand and solve problems and, therefore, their individual and collective potential for creativity and innovation. Emotional intelligence determines the qualities of the relationships. Relationships built on unconditional trust reduce the emotional complexity and type of tension (creative vs. emotional) between the people and frees their energy for concentrating on critical issues.

Figure Two

62

How is Diversity Related to Complexity and Creativity?

The only creative space in the universe is the space between differences—different ideas, perspectives, and opinions. This creative space is potentially (creative) tension-filled and chaotic. It is a "vacuum" in which new ideas and understandings are fertilized, incubated, and grown. New ideas and understandings, born of the many expressed ideas and knowledge inherent in the system, generate the potential to achieve great things through innovation and creativity, in response to societal needs and challenges.

Complexity and Creative Space

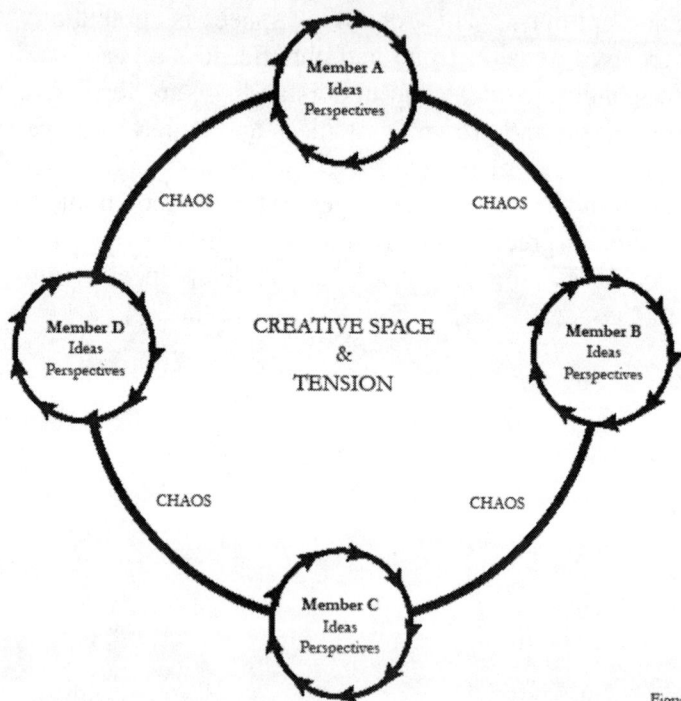

The only creative space in the universe is the space between differences (different ideas, perspectives, and opinions). This creative space is potentially tension-filled and chaotic— a "vacuum" in which new ideas and understandings are grown. New ideas and understandings born of the many expressed ideas and knowledge inherent in the system are built on unconditional trust.

How Do We Attain Greater Levels of Complexity?

Multiculturalism is about groups and group differences. While the multicultural approach seeks to duplicate perceived "societal complexity" in terms of group diversity, it offers limited complexity in terms of individual differences. The trick is to achieve "societal levels" of group diversity and then actively seek to transform group diversity into individual diversity and differences, thereby achieving a greater level of complexity than the society we serve. In order to attain greater levels of complexity, we must find ways to transform group (multicultural) complexity to individual (plural) diversity and complexity. The objective is to encourage, solicit, enable, and reward individuals who evolve away from the grips of the various groups to freely associate and express individual opinions, perspectives, and ideas that enrich the knowledge base of the organization. This enriched knowledge base greatly improves our ability to understand and respond to societal needs and challenges. It is from this knowledge base that collective intelligence, innovation, and creativity are born.

The beginning point of this transformative process is the shared vision and core set of values that represent common aspirations (commonalities) that rally and realign everyone for a paradigm shift that loosens (ethnic and racial) intra-group bonds with the purpose of facilitating interpersonal relationships across differences. As a group of people work together towards common goals, with a commitment to mutual support, they will also grow together emotionally, the practical effect of which is lowering divisive emotional barriers and free the individual, with his or her unique experiences, ideas, and perspectives, to enrich the knowledge base of the organization. This will enable our collective ability to understand and solve difficult social issues and problems.

What Are the Challenges of Multiculturalism?

The greater the complexity in an organization, the greater the potential for innovation and creativity. The capacity to respond to the complex challenges and needs of the community lies in a paradigm shift in our mental models. In general, our mental models are at the group level. That is why we continually conceptualize diversity-related problems in group terms. Multicultural organizations, because they conceptualize diversity in group terms, tend to have *intergroup* problems that are frequently referred to as *race relations problems.* Not surprising, as a remedy, race relations dialogue (or group) sessions are sponsored as solutions to perceived intergroup problems. Because of this mental model, organizations frequently perceive *interpersonal* problems as *intergroup problems.* That is why in *multicultural* organizations, there are seldom any reported incidents of *interpersonal* problems between black and white individuals. They do not have the appropriate mental models that enable them to distinguish individual action and behavior from that of the group.

Multicultural organizations report abundant *intergroup* and *race relations* problems. The reports they publish capture the data in group terms, but on closer inspection, most of the incidents buried in the group reports are interpersonal problems between individuals. When problems are misdiagnosed, the prescription to remedy the problems never works. Similarly, when we seek to understand problems with the wrong mental models, we tend to misdiagnose the problem and prescribe the wrong remedy, as illustrated in the following statement by William Anton, PhD, in *What's in a Name?*

In reflecting on the continued division between groups in our society and the increasing polarization of human relationships I made a few observations and parallels that may be useful in gaining perspective on what seems to be contributing to this negative period in our lives. It seems that at least part of the problem has to do with the way we label things. For example, the politically supported tendency to label things too narrowly can not only divert our attention from correct identification of problems but actually contribute to them by diverting resources needed to address the problem effectively and hence contribute to its solution. For example, the focus on "isms" such as racism, sexism, ageism, etc. as opposed to the broader concept of tyranny leads to fragmentation, misidentification and improper intervention. Not that these issues are unimportant but they are simply too symptomatic, narrow and polarizing to call forth the right solution for the right problem. An analogy to the human body might help to clarify this point. An intrinsic tumor might produce a number of symptoms—fever, pain, depression, etc.— that in the early stages of the process may be identified as the problem rather than symptomatic of the problem. What is worst, a great deal of time and energy may be spent treating the ostensible problem (i.e. symptoms) to little or no avail. Even more important however, the underlying disease process is allowed to flourish unabated as stronger and stronger medicine is applied to the symptoms that fail to improve or resolve. In fact, one of the great ironies is that the failure of symptoms to ameliorate is offered as evidence not of the misdiagnosis but of the tenacity of the problem. The consequence is that the malignity of the real problem (i.e. tyranny) not only remains unopposed but becomes an ally in the service of exorcising the symptoms once and for all; "Fighting fire with fire". This is not unlike the familiar protocol of using cancer-producing treatments to eradicate cancer cells. At best this is a short-term approach. The real victim is ultimately the body (i.e. ourselves) that must not only endure the iatrogenic consequences of symptomatic treatment (i.e. anger, rage) and the nurtured disease process (i.e. malignant response to malignant problem) but must witness the demise of the body (i.e. community) that is now at war with itself. As long as the organs of the body fight each other for resources that could be used to wage war against the real assailant, then the body itself will ultimately lose and the organs will simply die one by one. On the other hand, if we label things properly, then tyranny will be opposed wherever it occurs and in whatever form it manifests itself and can never be used by one group to enslave another. The enemy is tyranny itself not just delimited recognizable forms (recall "the devil can quote scriptures for his purpose"). The real disease is manifest all around us and we are guided to ignore its pervasiveness not only because of familiarity but also because we are taught what to fear by others who often embrace us in the service of their own political ends.[5]

How Do Fear and Trust Affect Complexity?

When fear is introduced as the transformative catalyst, the result is exponential and volatile complexity. Too much negatively charged energy arising from fear can lead to too many high intensity conflicts that degenerate into anarchy. Unconditional trust, on the other hand, has the opposite effect. When unconditional trust is the transformative catalyst, people generate the right type and amount of energy, which builds authentic relationships and allows the people to function effectively and achieve amazing results within the chaos of complexity. 6

Unconditional trust is the key to the quality and type of relationships that are co-created in our organizations and communities. Because of the negative interpersonal and individual dynamics that fear, distrust, and mistrust create, without unconditional trust, fear transforms complexity into anarchy. Without unconditional trust, the system of relationships that develops will be determined by fear and its manifestations of distrust and mistrust. Fear, distrust, and mistrust undermine relationships and lead to systemic fragmentation and disintegration. Fear retards the development of trusting relationships.

Complexity + fear = anarchy/disintegration.

Complexity + unconditional trust = chaos/creativity and innovation.

What Is the Difference Between Anarchy and Chaos?

Anarchy is a process by which systems, organizations, societies, communities, and organizations disintegrate. It is the polar opposite of chaos. Chaos is inherent in all creative and innovative processes. In chaos there is constancy in the type and pattern of relationships as structures and roles change to adapt to changing environmental conditions. In anarchy, there is a complete breakdown of relationships, structures, and roles. Anarchy is inherent in degenerative and destructive processes.

Chaos contains the inherent potential for anarchy in all transformative and generative processes, particularly if the relationships between the individuals are not the required pattern and type. The required pattern is a network system (not patchwork), and the type is authentic relationships (not coercive or utility) built on unconditional trust.

Chapter 5

Deal with Personal Prejudice

Judgments are a fact of life and are the basis of decision making. By *judgment*, I mean coming to conclusions about what something means, who you think someone is, or what they mean, not *judgment* in the biblical or legal sense. All of the disciplines have one key goal: recognizing stereotypes and dealing with personal prejudices.

By recognizing stereotypes and dealing with personal prejudices, you will ensure that when you do make judgments about others, those judgments are based on your experience with that individual and a genuine need to act. Realize that when you make judgments about others before you get to know them, you have pre-judged them. *Pre-judgment* is the source of the word *prejudice*. When you believe or assume every individual of a particular ethnicity, race, religion, gender, or sexuality, or any other category or group, is the same, you stereotype the individual.

When you believe groups of people are the same or similar, you have prejudices. Prejudice keeps you from knowing people as individuals, from discovering new ideas, new ways of thinking, and new ways of being, as well as limiting your potential and possibilities.

Prejudice can also lead you to hurt others through discrimination. Discrimination occurs when you treat people in a particular way based on their membership in some category, even if it is just "people like that," and is by no means limited to race and ethnicity. Ultimately, we all make judgments based on too little information from time to time. Nonetheless, it is necessary to be diligent about recognizing and eliminating prejudgments and stereotypes in order to be interpersonally effective.

When you practice impulse management, you will slow down the speed with which you make judgments about others and decrease the need for judgments.

Chapter 6

Build Relationships Across Differences

Forget the *patchwork* metaphor inherent in multiculturalism and its associated cultural competency for building intergroup relations. Think systemically and work to build a *network* system of interpersonal relationships across racial, ethnic, social, religious, and gender differences. A patchwork is a weaker concept metaphorically, because just as in multiculturalism, when pressure is applied to the figurative patchwork of relationships, the fabric will rip right along the points that connect the different colored pieces of fabric. But in a network system, it can be argued that pressure literary strengthens the relationship system at the points of connection between the individuals. An organization or society that is characterized by network systems (pattern) of authentic relationships (type) generates sustainable power that leads to innovations and creativity. 1

This is why you need to be open to developing friendships with others who appear different from you. When you have embodied the disciplines of emotional intelligence and authenticity, your social intelligence quotient will improve. This will translate to a greater ability to connect at the interpersonal level with people across differences, and will lead to the creation of a network system of relationships that will, collectively and individually, provide greater resources for creativity and innovation. The strength and complexity of your network of relationships is ultimately the strength of organizations and communities and your place in them.

The quality of the relationships between the people in the organization will determine the relationship system they co-create, their capacity for collaboration, their collective intelligence and potential for creativity and innovation. Emotional and social intelligence determine the quality of the relationships and type of power they collectively generate.

Why a Network Pattern?

A shift from patchwork to network pattern is essential. A network is a nonlinear (across differences) pattern of relationships. [2] A network is more pressure resistant and more sustainable than the metaphorical patchwork, because it creates a more integrated system of relationships that becomes even stronger under pressure. The strength of the network depends on not just the pattern but also the type of relationships across differences. Authentic network systems of relationships tend to generate authentic power and communities. The emotional qualities of the individuals in the organization determine the qualities of their interactions. The qualities of the interactions determine the qualities of the systems that they co-create, which, in turn, determines the type of power the system they co-create will generate.

Why Authentic Relationships?

Authentic relationships are the result of interactions that are trusting, respectful, honest, truthful, fair, caring, open, and forgiving. When this type of interaction is combined with a network pattern of interpersonal relationships across differences, a network system of authentic relationships leads to the creation of an authentic community of individuals. This is the most desirable and sustainable type of relationship because systemic integration through the network system co-creates what Martin Buber calls *"I – Thou relationships,"*[3] and subject-to-subject relationships in which people treat each other as subjects and not objects of manipulation and control. Authentic relationships and communities are co-created by interdependent people who contribute the most sustainable system and generate power within organizations; authentic power is the power to accomplish things with each other.

What Are Other Types of Systemic Relationships?

Coercive relationships are the results of interactions that are threatening, abusive, violent, or controlling within the organization. The chance exists that these types of behaviors are the result of unresolved issues from some past traumatic event. Depending on the intensity, these behaviors may be symptomatic of either post traumatic stress disorder or post traumatic stress syndrome.

Coercion breeds fear, which is infectious and can lead

to anger, mistrust, dishonesty, blaming, disrespect, and conflict. You should avoid these types of behaviors as much as possible. The norm in such situations is "Survival of the strongest"—usually those who have a monopoly on the means of coercion, which Blaine Lee in *The Power Principles* calls, *"the power to do things to others."* [4] Such behaviors create a coercive system of relationships that generate coercive power. These types of relationships are co-created by *independent* people in organizations. The type of power generated is unsustainable and undesirable because it eventually leads to systemic fragmentation and degeneration, always with the potential for anarchy. Martin Buber calls these types *"I-It Relationships,"* [5] the result of subject-to-object relationships in which one person is the subject to be feared and the other an object to be threatened and controlled.

Utility relationships are the result of interactions that are manipulative and deceptive, all in the interest of using people for personal gain. They are contagious and generate a system of relationships in which people use each other. The norm in such circumstances is *"You scratch my back, I scratch your back."* These types of relationship are co-created by codependent people who live and work together and willingly use each other for selfish personal gains. These relationships are unsustainable because they eventually end in win-lose situations and eventually create distrust, animosity, resentment, and conflict. Keep in mind that *coalition building* 5 eventually leads to systemic fragmentation and degeneration, always with the potential for anarchy.

As with coercive relationships, Martin Buber calls relationships that manipulate and deceive *"I-It Relationships."* A system in which there is mutual manipulation might be called *"It-It Relationships,"* or object-object relationships—none of which is sustainable.

What Is Authentic Power?

Authentic power (the power to do things with others) is the potential that authentic relationships create in authentic systems that define authentic communities.

What Is a System?

A system is composed of interdependent elements that interact to achieve a shared purpose or common goal. Systems thinking require you to:

- Think holistically in an integrated and interdependent way
- Realize that systems are relationships and vice versa
- Realize that the quality of the interactions between the parts determine the quality of the relationship, the system, and the outcome of their collective efforts
- Recognize that we co-create all our experiences and that systems work when everyone is responsible and accountable for the part that he or she contributes
- Recognize that actions taken in one part have repercussions for every other part of the system
- Focus on systemic change when there is a

problem, rather than blaming someone
- Recognize that systems breakdown at the points of connection between the parts 6

Chapter 7

Manage Differences Before They Become Conflicts

Manage differences, confusion, and misunderstandings before they become conflicts. When people who are culturally and racially different work together, the potential exists for misunderstandings and confusion to occur. Confusion and misunderstandings lead to conflict only if you rush to judgment. Discipline means suspending your assumptions and judgment when problems begin to arise and asking questions for clarification. Suspending your assumptions and judgments is more or less the same thing as adopting an "I don't know" stance instead of an "I know" stance.

The greater the intensity of your feelings, the more they are about you. When you experience intense feelings, it may be wise to withdraw from the conflict temporarily and reflect on your response. How are you projecting your values and beliefs onto other(s)? What assumptions are you making about their intentions, and what kind of judgments are you making about them? We all make assumptions and judgments; you couldn't communicate if you didn't. It is important during times of potential misunderstanding and conflict for you to be aware of the assumptions and judgments you make. Then you can deal with the real source of the misunderstanding or conflict.

When conflict does arise, seek first to understand the other person before you ask the other person to understand your concerns and points. [1]

Remember that you do not understand them until they say you understand.

How Does One Manage Misunderstanding and Conflict?

Misunderstandings about what people say and mean will occur. Confusion about why people behave the way they do will also occur. Managing differences, misunderstanding, and confusion before they become conflict requires:

- Suspending immediate assumptions, evaluations, and judgment when problems begin to arise in conversations or meetings

- Asking questions for additional information and clarification instead of making judgments about the intents of others based on assumptions

- Counting to ten before you respond when something goes wrong, in order to slow down so that you can respond instead of *react*

Always respect yourself and others

Respect yourself and present yourself well. When you respect yourself, you tend to respect others and, in turn, receive their respect. Remember that you must respect the dignity and worth of others if you wish your dignity and worth respected. The golden rule is old, rooted in the timeless wisdom that you set an example with your own conduct. As you learn and practice self-mastery, your confidence and emotional intelligence will increase. As your self-respect grows, so will your self-mastery, and vice versa, so that eventually you will establish a cycle of improvement where each characteristic feeds off the other.

Be open about how you feel. Recognize your feelings and express them in a responsible way. If you are angry, say, "I am angry," and be prepared to explain why. Do not suppress, deny, or act out the anger, because it will likely damage your relationships and lead you to conflict instead of a conversation so you can work things out. If you are uncertain about how to express your feelings responsibly, withdraw from the situation and think it through; if the feeling persists, discuss it once you have had a chance to think about it.

Do not act out the anger by swearing, cursing, blaming, or physically and verbally attacking others; that is professionally destructive, damaging relationships and undermining trust. If you need help identifying and expressing your feelings in a responsible way, you can ask a trusted friend or a professional for help.

How Do You Deal With Feelings of Anger In a Respectful Way?

To deal with anger in a respectful way, you must:
- Recognize your feelings

- Be open about your feelings and express them in a responsible way
- Learn to say *"I am angry"* when you are angry
- Avoid suppressing, denying, or acting out the anger by swearing, blaming, or physically and verbally attacking others because it will likely damage relationships and lead to a fight instead of a conversation where you can work out the conflict;
- Withdraw from the situation when you are uncertain about how you feel or how to express your feelings responsibly, think it through, and if the feeling persists, discuss it once you have had a chance to think about it

ℬↄↃℭℛ

Anger

To be angry is the easiest thing to do. But to be angry With the right person for the right reason at the right time in the right way— that people don't know how to do.

-- Aristotle

ℬↄↃℭℛ

- Seek help from a friend or professional if you need assistance identifying and expressing your feelings in a responsible way

Remember that it is possible that the more intense your feelings, the less they have to do with others and the issues of the moment. The intensity means your responses are more about you and your past. Emotional intelligence, however, does not mean never fighting. This is a misunderstanding that has its origin in pacifist philosophy. There are times when you may need to fight to preserve your life, job, property, and liberty, particularly when your rights, worth and dignity are being violated. To be effective, you must learn how, when, and when not to fight. You cannot afford to fight every conceivable battle. Life is not a war unless you are in the military.

Even in the military, soldiers know that they fight only when commanded to follow such an order. They are not at war every moment of the day or week. This said, knowing when and how to fight means using the right strategy for the right fight at the right time and knowing who you are fighting. So, exercise good judgment and fight wisely and only when you have no choice.

Chapter 8

Do Your Best to Keep All Commitments

Follow through on your commitments, including promises, agreements, and commitment to do or not do something. Make commitments only when you intend to keep them, and always keep them after you have made them. When you fulfill your commitments, others will respect and trust you because people who honor their commitments have a reputation for having integrity. People will consider you to have integrity when they find you to be reliable. Likewise, when you are reliable because you have integrity, people trust and respect you.

The greatest challenge to keeping commitments is having the wisdom to know what commitments you do not wish to or are unable to keep and the courage not to make them. Emotional intelligence is sometimes saying no to people you want to like you, people you are afraid of, and people with power over you. In the long run they are more likely to like you and be kind and generous to you because you have proven that you are reliable when you do make a commitment. Over time they will develop a perception of you as someone with integrity because you have had the wisdom to not make commitments you cannot or do not wish to keep. Once you develop the ability to say "no," you will find that keeping the commitments you do make is quite easy. [1]

What Is The Greatest Challenge To Keeping Commitments?

The greatest challenge to keeping commitments is having the judgment to know what commitments we do not wish to or are unable to keep and the courage not to make them.

Make commitments only when you mean to keep them, and always keep them after you have made them. If things change and you find out later that you can no longer keep a commitment, let others know what has changed and why you can no longer keep a commitment you made earlier. Always ask for understanding and forgiveness for changing your mind. Some people may not like the change, but they will respect and trust you for being open and honest.

If you find it difficult making and keeping commitments, we encourage you to revisit the process of self-mastery to get to the root of the problem. The chance exists that the difficulty you are having with commitment may be related to trust and forgiveness regarding something in your past experiences.

Chapter 9

Practice Personal Accountability

Know what you are responsible for at work. Be clear about what is expected of you and take responsibility for doing and being your best. Be accountable for the quality of your work and interactions. Admit mistakes or errors openly and truthfully. Similarly, be proud of and take credit for good work and meaningful interactions. Openly share your successes and accomplishments, and gracefully accept compliments. This may seem vain, but when it is balanced by admission of your mistakes, people will perceive you as honest and humble. The hardest person for you to be accountable to is you. For many reasons we deny our successes and failures. Once you have mastered the ability to be honest with yourself about these things, being accountable to others will be easy.

Remember to resist the temptation to blame others for your problems and mistakes. Blaming leads to hostility and distrust and is a projection of one's own doubts and fears about one's self onto others; the more certain you are it is "their" fault, the more likely you are projecting. Personal accountability means taking responsibility for the quality of your work and your interactions with others. Remember that you yourself may be the reason you are having problems getting along with others.

What Are the Elements of Accountability?

There are two elements to personal accountability:

1. Personal responsibility means knowing what we are each responsible for at work and at home. It means being clear about what is expected of us at work and in our interpersonal relationships and taking responsibility for doing and being our best.

2. Personal accountability means accounting honestly and truthfully for the quality of our work and interactions. This means openly admitting mistakes or errors. We must also be proud of and take credit for good work and meaningful interactions.

Accountability also means resisting the temptation to blame others for our problems and mistakes.

What are the accountability questions?

When something goes wrong at work or in our relationships, it is advisable to begin by asking ourselves three fundamental questions that are essential for personal accountability:

1. What is really happening here?
2. What have I contributed to it?
3. What can I do now to change it to the outcome that I want?

Examples of Accountable Behaviors
Example One:

You are having problems getting along with a coworker, Sue.

*"Why is **Sue** so difficult to work with?"* or
*"Why is **she** such a bitch?"* or
*"When are **they** going to do something about her nasty attitude and behavior?"*

Instead of thinking and complaining about Sue, recognize that your attitude is key to asking the accountable questions that will improve your ability to work with Sue. Ask yourself the following questions:

> *"How can **I** improve my ability to work well with Sue?"*
> *"What can **I** do differently to enable me to work well with Sue?*

Example Two

You are having problems with one of your employees. You desperately want to improve the situation and end the problems, which HR has recommended. What questions should you begin to ask yourself as you struggle to find a solution to the problems *you* are having?

Why am **I** really having problems with my employee?

What am *I* contributing to the problems?
What can *I* do **right now** to change the
situation to get the results that I want?

Example Three

You are having problems with your supervisor.
You desperately need to improve the situation
and end the problems before you lose your job,
which HR has advised you to do. What questions
should you begin to ask yourself as you struggle
to find a solution to the problems that *you* are
having?

Why am *I* really having these problems with
my supervisor?
What am *I* contributing to the problems?
What can *I* do **right now** to change the
situation to get the results that I want?

Accountable Thinking:

*"I realize that my success depends on my ability to work
well with my employees and coworkers. The next time I
interact with them, I will try to be more aware of my
feelings, behavior, and actions so that I may understand
what I am doing to make it difficult to work together.
When I determine what new behaviors will help me
interact more effectively with them, I will make the
appropriate behavioral changes. I want to be successful and
am committed to doing the right thing."*

John Miller, the motivational speaker and author of works on personal accountability, writes in *The Question Behind the Question: a Tool to Point You Down the Accountable Path:*

"The QBQ (Question Behind the Question) is the accountable question which can be found behind most any other question you ask in life. It's the question that puts you in charge, gives you the energy to act, and ensures that the actions you take will be accountable ones." [1]

He identifies the QBQ guidelines for asking action questions that lead to personal accountability:

1. A QBQ usually starts with the word *what* or the word *how*. What can I do to help this situation? How should I proceed in solving this problem? The *what* and *how* keep you focused on your choices and your action. The word *why*, on the other hand, often leaves you powerless and rarely gets you anywhere.

2. A QBQ always contain *I*. It is the *I* which keeps you from dwelling on things outside of your control. *I* keeps you focused on your *contributions* and *concerns*. The word *you* points outward, but *I* stays right at home.

3. A QBQ focuses on action. It's the *action* you take as a result of asking accountable questions that makes all the difference. [2]

Chapter 10

Be Fair with Yourself and Others

You must reflect on decisions that you make that directly affect others, particularly those decisions that affect the people who live, learn, and work with and for you. Each important decision you make must pass the fairness test. [1] Before you can really be fair with anyone else, you must first be fair with yourself. If you find it difficult being fair with others, it may be because you have not forgiven yourself and others who may have hurt you. When we fail to forgive ourselves and others, we tend to find it difficult to trust. When we do not trust, we tend not to be fair. In other words, to be fair you need to forgive the past and learn to trust unconditionally. You do not have to be angry to protect yourself from harm—you need to become smarter. Anger may make you physically stronger, but it does not make you smarter.

One way to forgive the past and learn to trust unconditionally is to practice self-awareness through self-examination, so that you can begin to understand what makes you tick emotionally, which leads to the motivation for self-discipline, forgiveness, and self-mastery.

Develop Standards of Fairness

Develop standards as part of your fairness test by identifying objective criteria to guide your decisions, particularly, if you are in a supervisory position, those that affect who gets recognized, rewarded, and promoted and who gets professional development opportunities. Set objective criteria for making decisions that could reasonably lead anyone to the same decision. Ensure that your decision or conclusion meets the following fairness standards:

- Be aware and conscious of the biases, prejudices, past experiences, and pain that may adversely impact your decisions and actions
- Treat employees and others as you wish to be treated
- Be equitable in your treatment of everyone, including employees with performance challenges, particularly those you don't like
- Ensure that your decisions are fair and are based on verified facts, not the opinions and desires of others
- In the final analysis, *do no harm* should be your guiding motto. [2]

To pass the fairness test, ask yourself the following questions:
- Were I in this person's position, would I find this decision fair and equitable?
- Were this person someone else, would I reach the same conclusion or make the same decision? Would I have made the same decision were he a high performer or someone I like?

93

- Do I really have all of the facts and information I need to take this action or make this judgment or decision?
- Would anyone else looking at the same facts reach the same conclusion or arrive at the same decision?
- How will this judgment, decision, action, or conclusion affect the individual?

Fairness standards are critical to building trust and maintaining your integrity. One way to do this is to get everyone involved in defining fairness and engaged in identifying fairness standards for the group or family. When members of a group have been involved in determining the standards of fairness for themselves and the workplace, such an inclusive process may allow everyone to share a sense of fairness.

Encourage Openness and Engagement

During meetings, fairness also means ensuring balance and inclusion in deliberations. Seek to maintain balance in conversations and meetings by asking questions contrary to positions already posited to ensure an issue is fully explored and understood. Take contrary positions to challenge yourself and others to explore other options or perspectives.

If you are a supervisor, strive to be inclusive, and encourage everyone to engage during conversations and meetings. Maintain fairness so that the conversations are not dominated by one person or group to the exclusion of others; in your comments, avoid showing preference for one person or group. Pose questions and problems to the group and ask for input and suggestions from them before you make decisions or arrive at conclusions about major decisions. Ensure that you not sending subtle negative signals that either you don't like or do prefer a person or course of action. Encourage those who are quiet, reserved, or withdrawn to join in and contribute to the conversations, and manage the aggressive, dominant, and talkative people so that everyone has a fair chance to contribute to the conversations. 3

Chapter 11

Listen Carefully for Understanding

It takes personal discipline to carefully observe, listen, and ask for clarification and additional details. When you are speaking, you understand your unspoken connections, assumptions, and reasons for what you are saying and how you are saying it. However, when you listen to others you do not have access to those unspoken elements. Some of the time, that is not a problem. Much of the time, however, our unspoken connections, assumptions, and reasons are not the same as they are for others. Asking questions that clarify or request more detail helps you avoid misunderstandings. Likewise, realize that others do not have the benefit of knowing your unspoken connections, assumptions, and reasons for what you are saying and how you are saying it. It is a fact of life, not an indicator that others are stupid, ignorant, inattentive, mean, uninterested, or careless.

It is always safer to assume you do not know than to assume you do know. There is no real risk in this assumption. Think of it as delaying your response. Slow down, listen, and think, and remember that everybody makes sense to him- or herself. Understanding comes from asking probing questions to gain information and clarity and to confirm your assumptions.

Give others your full attention. Avoid rushing to

judgment about what is being said until you have enough information. When you think you have enough information, you are probably wrong and need to listen some more. We always come to conclusions about others faster than we do about ourselves.

Why Ask Questions?

Remember to ask questions, because they will help you better understand what others are saying and provide a knowledge base on which to make sound decisions. Ask questions to:

- Get additional information
- Clarify the issues
- Check your understanding

What Are the Benefits of Careful Listening?

Because stress has a profound effect on a person's listening ability, the average person can only take between 15 and 20 percent of the available information—one of the ways stress makes people stupid. Disciplining yourself to asking questions for clarification enables you to take in additional information, above the 15 percent perceived by most people. Imagine what you could accomplish if you could take in 50 percent of the information from your conversations, meetings, and trainings. Margaret Wheatley tells us that information informs and forms the organization and its people. [1]

When you are able to discipline yourself emotionally, you will become more intelligent and effective, because you develop greater capacity levels to:

- Take in information beyond the average of 15 percent intake level
- Understand people, problems, and issues
- Solve problems
- Be creative and innovative
- Manage differences and misunderstandings before they become conflicts

Remember, if you have problems listening or asking questions during conversations and meetings, it may be because of anxiety or chronic stress, which are usually the result of some traumatic experience.

Chapter 12

Give and Receive Feedback with Care

Giving feedback refers to the act of telling others about your assessment of what they have done. There are two basic types of feedback: positive and negative. Providing positive feedback is quite easy. When done appropriately giving positive feedback can strengthen your relationship and reinforce confidence—yours and theirs.

On the other hand, providing negative feedback is very difficult. When not done appropriately, it can lead to mistrust, fear, and conflict. Remember to focus on the problem or behavior, not the person. If you find that you want to give feedback out of anger, frustration, resentment, or revenge, withdraw and think about it. As we have pointed out before, the stronger your feelings, the more they are about you.

When you are open to positive feedback you feel confident; your self-esteem, the quality of your work, and your satisfaction with relationships are enhanced. But remember that your ability to learn, grow, and change is also directly tied to your capacity to be open to negative criticism.

Many people are not very effective at giving negative feedback. So when you are receiving negative feedback, it is important to know that if the person doing so seems critical, judgmental, or angry toward you as a person, that criticism, judgment or anger is based in their fears and lack of interpersonal skills. Try to listen through that tone for useful feedback about how you can do things better and ignore the parts that seem personal, if you wish to continue to grow and avoid being drawn into unnecessary conflicts. When you allow such behavior to make you angry because of the way feedback was provided, remember that your response in such a situation tends to becomes self-righteous.

Providing Constructive Feedback

Feedback is essential in any work environment. Employees need to know when they are on track and when they are not. It is important to examine your motives and intentions before giving feedback. Remember that whether positive or negative, feedback is more effective when it is given in a timely manner, preferably soon after the event or problem. Bruce Tulgen tells in his book *FAST Feedback,* that feedback is best when it is frequent, accurate, specific, and timely. [1]

What is your reason for giving feedback?

Is it genuinely a chance to help the employee learn, or is it a way to assert your authority or retaliate for something? Feedback that comes out of benevolent motives is more apt to be accepted positively. Once you are clear that your feedback is truly constructive, try the following tips:

- Be careful; criticize in private, not public

- Be specific about what you like and don't like and about points of agreement
- Be descriptive, not emotional
- Focus on the issues, problems, or behaviors, not the person. Always respect the worth and dignity of the person.
- Be tactful; begin with the positive, or what you like and agree with, before giving negative feedback

Chapter 13

Be Flexible and Open to New Ideas

While it is important that you clearly express your ideas and opinions, be careful not to become attached to them. It is often difficult to separate our opinions and ideas from our selves, but we must. If someone opposes your ideas and opinions, it has nothing to do with you, even if they think it does. When you become too attached to your ideas and opinions, you become predisposed to defending them (i.e., defending yourself). When you are busy defending your ideas and opinions, you are not listening to others. Likewise, others don't listen to you when you get defensive, because when you get defensive, other people will usually become defensive in response to your defensiveness. Ideas are never in conflict, they are just different, and that is good. People are in conflict over ideas when they feel the need to defend them because they have become

ಬಿಶ

Flexibility

Remember that things are not always as they appear neither are they otherwise.

- *Buddhist saying*

ಬಿಶ

one with their ideas. Do not make the mistake of translating "something is wrong" into "someone is wrong."

Why Is Assertiveness Essential to Flexibility?

When you are assertive, you tend to be flexible, just as when you are aggressive you tend to be rigid. Being assertive and flexible in your conversations opens up options and creates room for possibilities with others, leading to collaboration. Aggressiveness and rigidity close down options and possibilities, diminishing your ability to listen, which results in your inability to learn, understand others, and change. If you are unaware of whether you are rigid and aggressive, spend a few moments completing the Basic Emotional Intelligence Profile (Appendix 2) with a few people who work with you; pay attention to the Flexibility scale. If you are aware that you tend to be rigid and aggressive, it may be because you have problems with trust and forgiveness. Use the self-mastery process to find out why this is so and commit to doing something about it. Remember that flexibility and assertiveness are signs of confidence in your ability to work well with others. [1]

What are the essential disciplines for flexibility?

- Listen and observe carefully to take in information
- Ask questions for clarification to take in even more information

- Suspend assumptions, certainty, and evaluation
- Be assertive, not aggressive or passive
- Value different opinions and ideas
- Slow down the conversation
- Collaborate and discover new understandings, possibilities, and solutions

Chapter 14

Being Your Best at What You Do

Strive to be your best at everything you do, particularly what you do for a living. This means you must be aware of your strengths and weaknesses. The only way you can do this is by being honest, truthful, and open with yourself. Again, you will not be able to do so unless you forgive yourself for past mistakes, commit to change, and learn what it will take to be your best on the job. To do this, you must also have a vision in your mind of what it means to be your best at what you do. Then take stock of what skills and disciplines you need to master in order to be your best. After that you must commit to the discipline, knowledge, and learning required to master new disciplines and skills essential to the vision you have for yourself. 1

It will take time to achieve your goals, because it takes perseverance and the commitment to practice and learn from the experience until you have mastered the core disciplines and learned the requisite skills and essential competencies. Sometimes a role model can help you formulate a personal vision. Look for someone in the same field or type of job you seek whom you believe has achieved the desired state of performance. To clarify your vision and determine what you need to do to be your best, observe that person. 2

What Are the Characteristics of Peak Performers?

Even if everyone thinks successful individuals are already great and may be among the best at what they do, they continue to learn, grow, and enhance their knowledge and skills. Research indicates that people who have achieved unconscious mastery (flow) have certain characteristics in common.

In general, peak performers tend to:
- Have a clear and compelling vision of themselves
- Have a clear understanding of their strengths and weaknesses
- Synchronize everything they do during the day that support their vision
- Can explain how they are frequently able to perform at peak levels
- Have a network of individuals who provide feedback, support, and encouragement, particularly when the going gets rough
- Have the emotional resiliency to stay on track with their vision

How are they were able to achieve flow? When asked, they always reply, "I don't know. I just do it." This is because for them performance is beyond the level of unconscious competency; it is at the level of unconscious mastery. 3

How Does One Become a Peak Performer?

The type of vision that inspires peak performance comes from a burning desire deep within the individual. This desire creates and sustains your commitment to the vision and core set of values (authenticity) and to continual learning, growth, and development.

Research indicates that to become a peak performer, you must:

1. Discover your true purpose, talent, and passion
2. Commit to a compelling vision and core set of values
3. Develop your goals and a plan of action
4. Acknowledge the need for change and stay focused on your vision
5. Practice self-mastery and consistency
6. Be open to experimenting with new ideas and learning from mistakes
7. Stay connected to respected colleagues and esteemed mentors 4

Let us take a closer look at each of these seven key characteristics in terms of what you may have to do to become a peak performer in the diverse workplace.

To help you with each of the steps toward peak performance, here are some evocative questions for your reflection after each step.

1. Discover and acknowledge your purpose, passion, and talents

❖ *To what would you like to commit your life?*

The process of becoming a peak performer involves discovering your purpose, talent, and passion and committing to your core values and vision for your life. Purpose, vision, and values give you courage, direction, and meaning. Without knowing why you are on earth, what you believe, and what you want for your life, you cannot dream of becoming a peak performer. 5

a) Discovering your purpose in life

❖ *Why do you exist?*

This is about why you exist. You have a purpose in life, although you may not be consciously aware about it. We each have a purpose in life. By clarifying your purpose, you can become more conscious of the quality of your work and more authentic in how you relate to others.

b) Discovering your passion and talents

❖ *What type of work are you good at and love doing?*

Identify your passion and talents: something you really enjoy and love doing that makes you *come alive* inside; something you are really good at and want to become even better at. 6

2. Commit to a compelling vision and core set of values

❖ *What type of person or professional would you like to become?*

Envision the type of professional and person you would like to become. Your core set of values are about your actions and interactions from this day on as you strive to achieve your vision.

a) Developing your personal vision

❖ *What is your personal or shared vision?*

Steven Covey recommends that you *"begin with the end in mind"* as you decide on a vision for your life. In other words, decide what you would like to become when you grow up. 6

Imagine what type of job you would really enjoy—for example, becoming an emergency surgeon. Imagine in your mind's eye what kind of emergency surgeon you would like to become, or identify a role model you admire. The clearer the vision, the more achievable it becomes.

Keep clarifying your vision to the point that you can see yourself as the respectful and caring surgeon you have imagined. Find a profession that is attractive and imagine yourself in that role in the future, with the passion, talent, and knowledge to do an exceptional job. 7

b) Identifying and committing to your core set of values

❖ *How are you going to behave in your quest to become a peak performer?*

Values are about how you feel and behave as you strive to achieve your vision. Commit to a core set of values (unconditional trust, respect, truth, honesty, fairness, openness, care, and forgiveness) that are essential to being authentic.

> **℘**
>
> **Peak Performance**
>
> *"Peak performers adapt continually, learn from mistakes, and continually move forward toward their vision. Stubbornness and rigidity are not virtues in a creative world. Peak performers learn and adjust as they proceed. They are flexible."*
>
> --Tom Heuerman
>
> **℧**

- Build sustainable relationships that will enable your success as you strive to achieve your vision.

3. Develop your goals and pursue a plan

of action

❖ *What do you need to do to enable you to achieve your vision?*

Decide on the short- and long-term goals related to your vision by determining three to five things you need to do to enable you to achieve your vision.

a) Developing your goals

❖ *What specific actions do you need to take in the next few years to achieve your vision?*

The goals you identify must align with the qualifications, skills, and experiences essential to achieving your ultimate vision. Remember that peak performers are goal setters. Identify goals that inspire you to reach your ultimate vision.

Divide your goals into short-term goals (three to five years) and long-term goals (five to ten years).

b) Developing your action plans

❖ *When and how are you going to complete each of your goals?*

Develop a plan in your mind or on paper

with specific actions you need to take to achieve your vision. This will ensure that you "put first things first," as Steven Covey recommends in *Seven Habits of Highly Effective People.* [8]

4. Acknowledge the need for change and stay focused on your vision

❖ *What needs to change in your life or work that, if changed, would enable you to achieve your vision?*

a) Acknowledging the need for change

❖ *What benefit or cost would accrue to you if you do not change your performance and acquire new skills?*

Acknowledging the need for change is the beginning of the transformative process. The key to change is to have a clear vision of the future. Continually compare and assess where you currently stand in regard to that vision of the future.

This way you know exactly where change needs to occur, what needs to change, and the amount of change necessary for achieving your vision. What are you are now doing that is standing in the way of your vision, which you must stop doing?

Acknowledge the need for change and do whatever you can to change.

a) Staying focused on your vision

❖ *What are the current challenges and obstacles to staying focused on your vision?*

There will be emotional, as well as creative, challenges in your path. Some will appear insurmountable; others will be smaller. Staying focused on the vision is the key motivator to redirecting your emotional energy to assist you in overcoming these challenges.

5. Practice self-mastery and consistency

❖ *How are you feeling, and what is the quality of your performance?*

Self-mastery begins with self-awareness. Frequently check to ensure awareness of how you are feeling throughout the day and take some deep breaths, if needed, to change how you are feeling, always remembering to align feelings, thoughts, and actions with the desired outcome of your performance.

There is some empirical evidence suggesting a strong correlation between the level of emotional arousal and peak performance, particularly in relationship to functions that require high levels of concentration. The Yerkes-Dodson Law indicates that, up to a certain point, performance increases with emotional arousal. Beyond moderate level of arousal, performance effectiveness begins to decrease. The process is graphically illustrated by the bell curve below.

The highest level of arousal for any type of job is a moderate level of arousal. Beyond that, the individual will experience diminished levels of performance.

Take time during the day to check how you are doing and the quality of the work you are doing. How has your performance been lately? Has it been up to your expectations? Are you on the right track? What additional skills do you need that you did not anticipate? 9

Always remember to make sure that your feelings, thoughts, and actions are in alignment with the desired outcome of your performance and vision.

Emotional Arousal and Peak Performance

Peak performance is achieved when emotions flow between low- and mid-level arousal.

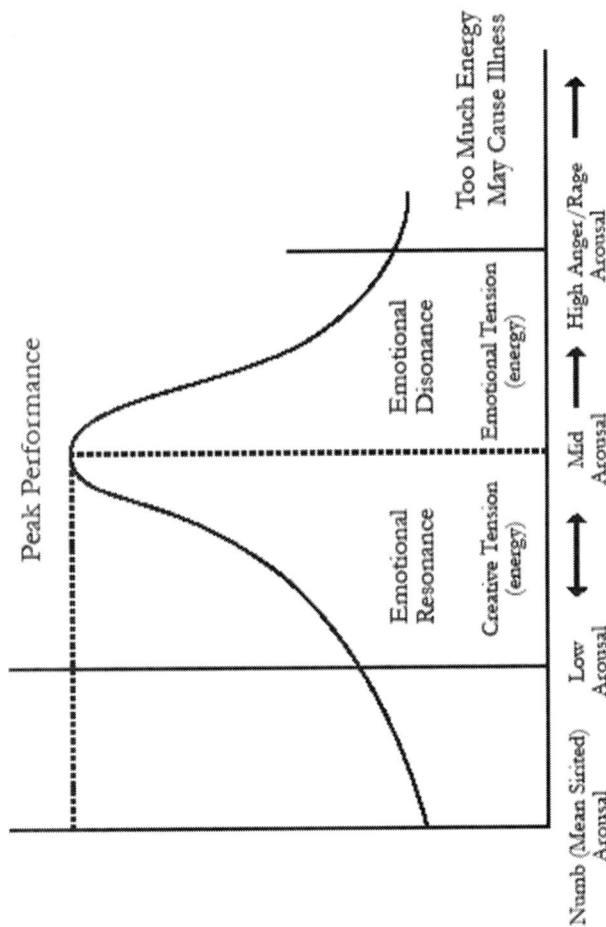

Peak Performance

Emotional Resonance

Emotional Dissonance

Creative Tension (energy)

Emotional Tension (energy)

Numb (Mean Spirited) Arousal

Low Arousal

Mid Arousal

High Anger/Rage Arousal

Too Much Energy May Cause Illness

Modified Yerkes/Dodson Law

Figure Four

Stay open to experimenting with new ideas, and learn from mistakes

❖ *What do you need to learn that will enable you to achieve your vision of becoming a peak performer?*

Become eternally curious, with a child's mind, for learning new things and asking questions; always search for new ideas, seek answers to challenges, and listen generatively to what others have to say.

Recognize that peak performers continually adapt and learn from their mistakes. As Tom Heuerman explains:

> *Peak performers continually learn from mistakes, and continually move forward toward their vision. Stubbornness and rigidity are not virtues in a creative world. Peak performers learn and adjust as they proceed. They are flexible.* [10]

6. Stay connected to respected colleagues and esteemed mentors.

❖ *What is your support system?*

These are esteemed colleagues and mentors who have in the past provided you selfless, valued advice and guidance; as a result, you know you can rely on them again to provide valued advice, guidance, and support, especially when the going gets rough, as it will in the future. These are people from whom you learn and seek advice and feedback to stay on vision track.

From Competency to Mastery (Flow)

Our feelings determine our behavior and performance in any given endeavor or professional field. Studies have shown that people who are great at what they do have some things in common. They are happy, they like and enjoy what they do, and they are always in a learning mode. They are constantly learning and growing, even when everyone around them believes they among the best at what they do. Work on your weaknesses, and they become strengths. Stop working on them, and they will again become weaknesses.

Levels of Peak Performance

It is a continual process of growth and development until you reach the state of performance Mihaly Csikszentmihalyi calls *flow*, a higher state of peak performance. Peak performance at the level of conscious competency is *good* performance. This encompasses people who are *very good* at what they do. *Great* performance, or *flow*, however, occurs at the level of unconscious mastery.

Steps to Peak Performance
From competency (good) to mastery (great!) and flow

How we feel determines how we behave and perform in any given endeavor or professional field.

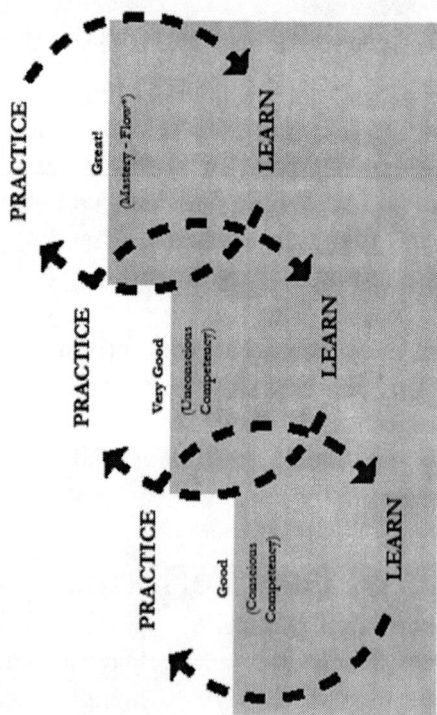

PRACTICE

PRACTICE

PRACTICE

PRACTICE

Great!
(Mastery - Flow*)

Very Good
(Unconscious Competency)

Good
(Conscious Competency)

LEARN

LEARN

LEARN

LEARN

*Reference: Flow: The Psychology of Optimal Experience by Mihaly Csikszentmihalyi (1990)

Figure Five

118

Conscious Competency: These people are good at what they do. To perform at this level, you must make an extraordinary conscious effort to direct all of your attention to focus on the task. The degree to which you can successfully align and synchronize cognitive (knowledge and skills), emotional (feelings), and physical functions (physical dexterity) will determine your level of performance and how well you accomplish the task. Conscious competency is the first level of performance that you must achieve in your quest to become a great performer, professionally or recreationally. It is a level that is essential to achieving improved levels of performance and the first stage in the natural progression from good to great performance.

However, because attaining focused attention and synchronicity requires disciplined energy and concentration, as well as the requisite level of knowledge and skills, some individuals are never able to achieve the next level of performance: unconscious competency. They remain recognizably good at what they do but never improve. Others do achieve temporary success at being good but then experience slowly declining performance as the stress of maintaining the status quo becomes unbearable. After achieving temporary performance success, others are overcome by scandals and ethical or legal troubles arising from repressing their pathologies until they can no longer successfully do so.

Others are unable to stay at this level of performance for a long period because they are unable to or disinterested growing their knowledge base as the need arises; they find it too difficult or are unable to achieve the level of focused attention necessary to move to the next level of performance.

To achieve lasting success you must deal with whatever emotional issues affect your ability to achieve focused attention and synchronicity. If you fail to do so, you will not graduate to the next performance level: unconscious competency.

Unconscious Competency: These people are very good at what they do. This level of performance is the result of a moderate amount of effort to achieve focused attention through emotional, cognitive, and physical synchronicity, along with attaining a greater knowledge base and the requisite skill-set to achieve very good work. In order to reach this level of performance, the individual has to consciously make an effort to pay careful and focused attention to the task. With focused attention, these individuals sometimes do great work, but performance is not as consistent as in the state of mastery, or flow, described below. In many case, failure to achieve a higher level of performance results from the lack of the requisite level of knowledge or skills, even though the person may be able to achieve a greater level of emotional, physical, and cognitive synchronicity than is required for performance at the level of conscious competency.

Unconscious Mastery: These people are great at what they do. Unconscious mastery means you are able, with very little or no effort or discipline, to quickly achieve a very high level of focused attention and emotional, cognitive, and physical synchronicity more frequently than persons who are at the levels of conscious competency and unconscious competency. Not only does it mean that you make little or no effort to achieve focused attention and synchronicity, this comes to you almost naturally. Flow means you are a superior performer with superior results most of the time, if not absolutely all of the time. Consistently performing at the peak performance results in flow.

Mihaly Csikszentmihalyi identified four critical attributes of the state of flow:

1. Focused Attention: Alignment of emotional, rational, and physical functions; attention is absolutely focused on the task at hand. The person is not distracted by anything.

2. Prepared: The person's skills and abilities are up to the task's demand.

3. Exceptional Performance: The person's performance is spectacular.

4. Rewarding Experience: A very exhilarating and rewarding state, where the person feels great, is really having fun, and enjoys the work he or she is doing.[12]

Epilogue

While we may not be responsible for the trauma of our birth and upbringing, we owe it to ourselves to heal the wounds from those experiences. Failure to heal those wounds invariably results in living with fear and distrust and may ultimately define who we are for the rest of our lives. Fear has the effect of diminishing work relationships, job performance, and effectiveness.

Such fear is responsible for 98 percent of social problems in the diverse workplace. Fear is the source of the mistrust and distrust that plagues our teams and saps team morale and energy, diminishing organizational potential. Fear undermines relationships and can negatively affect everything in organizations, including productivity, quality, safety, and security. That is why it is not uncommon in these days of increased workplace violence to hear employees admonished to keep their "emotions" out of the workplace, their decision-making, and their reward systems.

In fact "emotions" are often blamed for many of the diversity-related problems between employees and groups. As a result, organizational culture has evolved to become increasingly "dispassionate," where "reason" trumps "emotion" and decisions are made based on cold, hard facts and nothing else. We now train administrators and managers to make "data-driven decisions," supposedly devoid of any emotional considerations. With the evolution of this type of organizational culture, the workplace has become more heartless, mean-spirited, and toxic to the health of those who work in them. It seems the more dispassionate we strive to become, the greater the level of fear becomes, increasing the degree of mistrust and distrust between employees.

Because of this, the word "emotion" has come to represent all that is "negative" and "bad" in human behavior and organizations. From such a vantage point, "emotion" appears to be a one-dimensional problem. Yet we all know that emotion is not one-dimensional; the positive "good" emotions on the other side of the coin are fundamental to authentic, emotionally intelligent, and diverse organizations. The source of this "good" or positive emotion and one of the most powerful ideas that drives exceptional performance is unconditional trust. Unconditional trust is a powerful dynamic that can positively affect everything in organizations, including relationships, quality, productivity, and effectiveness.

But what if we were to view emotions in a different way altogether, as another kind of intelligence, beyond reason and logic? An intelligence that—if we could learn to access it—could become nothing short of a touchstone to increased collaboration, a higher level of influence with others, and greater productivity and effectiveness.

The fact is, such an intelligence exists; it is called emotional intelligence. Unheard of only a decade or so ago, in the past few years emotional intelligence, or EI, has become something remarkable—the centerpiece of mainstream organizational training.

Entire conferences are now devoted to discovering its secrets, and virtually everyone has an opinion about whether it is really "new" at all.

Emotions are intrinsic parts of our personalities—who we are—and crucial to developing quality working relationships and employee satisfaction. We can't leave emotions out of our work decisions, nor can we leave them back at home and pretend to be robots when we go to work. Emotions make us human and are essential to organizational effectiveness.

In fact, efforts to suppress emotions at work instead of mastering the impulses that drive negative behaviors guarantees emotional explosions at some time—usually when it is least expected. The result is always conflict, which depletes employee morale by negatively impacting organizational climate and, in extreme cases, drives workplace violence. 1.You have learned in this book that emotional intelligence is essential to personal and professional success in the diverse workplace and society. We have learned that human beings by nature are emotional, with the capacity to heal the emotional wounds that drive the impulses that prompt us in strained emotional situations to *react* instead of *respond*.

In addition, we have also learned that to be successful in the diverse and multicultural workplace, we must manage the emotional impulses that prompt us to react in order to develop the ability to become more responsive in a way that fosters authentic relationships across differences. This also means we have to work hard to become more unconditionally trusting, respectful, truthful, honest, fair, open, caring, and forgiving of ourselves and one another. Trust-driven behavior defines the qualities of the relationships we develop and the types of systems and energy we generate collectively.

As the pace of change in the diverse workplace accelerates in the future, we will all have to learn at the speed of change to stay effective, relevant, and successful in the diverse workplace. To achieve this, we will have to improve our emotional and social intelligence quotients and our capacity for continual self-renewal.

So don't drive emotions out of the workplace. Instead, discipline and harness them in order to transform your team and organization, and then achieve amazing levels of performance and excellence.

The core emotional disciplines of authenticity that you have learned in this book represent a high standard of behavior. The pursuit of these disciplines through practice can lead to improved personal relationships and professional performance. Remember that prejudices and stereotypes are held by all people and are not restricted to the traditional categories of race, ethnicity, national origin, gender, or sexual orientation. If you commit yourself to putting into practice the disciplines and behaviors discussed in this book, the result can be a whole new experience in building effective relationships and success in the diverse workplace. More importantly, you will find yourself open to learning, which means being open to possibilities for personal improvement that go far beyond the basic lessons of this book. Success in an authentic and diverse workplace requires emotional and social intelligence. Your careful reading and reflection in these areas has prepared you to take another step toward successfully using those multiple filters for emotional and social intelligence. Good luck to you.

Appendices

Appendix 1

Emotional Intelligence Quiz

Directions: This quiz is designed to help you assess your *basic level* of emotional intelligence (EI).

Just a tip: the degree to which this quiz can approximate your basic EI level depends on how closely your *response* or *reaction* approximates how you would normally behave in each scenario. Avoid thinking about your response and pay attention to the energy impulse that you will feel as you read through each scenario; allow the impulse to determine which box to check. Don't check the "right answer"—this is not a test with one right answer. Since each individual is different, quiz results will vary depending on the individual.

Please make a check mark in the box next to the answer that best reflects how you would respond in each scenario.

So, how emotionally intelligent are you? Let's find out.

1. During a team meeting, another colleague accuses you, in an angry tone of voice, of undermining his efforts related to a major project. What would you do?

   ❑ Politely ignore him because the best way to deal with angry people is to ignore them.
   ❑ Fight back angrily because if you do not, he will think you are a pushover.
   ❑ Speak up immediately by reminding the person that *his* behavior is inappropriate and demand an apology.
   ❑ Wait until after the meeting to speak privately with the person about *his* behavior.

2. You receive a telephone call from a very angry customer, who is cursing about a problem. What would you do?

   ❑ Tell the customer to calm down and ask her to stop yelling at you.
   ❑ Tell the customer that she is being unfair by taking out her anger on you, since you have done nothing wrong.
   ❑ Tell the customer that you understand her frustration and offer to help her resolve the problem.
   ❑ Hang up the telephone without saying anything.

3. You work in a department that is trying to reduce the amount of racial conflict in the office. You are present when an African American coworker

angrily makes generalized accusations about racism in your department. What would you do?

- Ignore it because African Americans are entitled to be angry about racism because they have suffered from racism for so long.
- Speak to the person privately and encourage the person to report any incidents of racism to the supervisor/manager or the EEO/Human Resources Office instead of making generalized allegations.
- Speak up immediately about racism and tell all whites that they need to take racial sensitivity training.
- Join in the condemnation of racism in the department and organize minorities to fight racism in the organization.

4. You heard from someone in another department that one of your team members has been quietly taking all the credit for the successful completion of a team project. What would you do?

- Publicly confront him and let everyone know that he doesn't deserve all of the credit for the accomplishments
- Through the use of innuendoes during your next team meeting, say something about how you despise unethical people who always take sole credit for team accomplishments.
- Speak with him privately about what you have heard and encourage him to share credit with the rest of the team for team accomplishments

- Quietly tell everyone in the team that he had taken sole credit for work done by the team.

5. You are a member of a team that has a coworker who is always making negative comments about your department manager/supervisor. What would you do?

- Publicly confront her behavior and remind her that such behavior is not in line with your organization's values and expected behaviors.
- Ignore the behavior and hope the person stops making negative comments about your manager/supervisor.
- After the meeting, speak privately with the person about the inappropriateness of such behavior and the effects of negative comments on the rest of the team.
- Quietly tell your manager/supervisor about the person's behavior and comments.

6. You encounter a team member who is extremely angry because he has just been publicly blamed by another team member for problems in a project they are working on. What would you do?

- Tell him to forgive and forget and not sweat the small stuff.
- Encourage him to quietly speak with the person about the problems and clarify any misunderstandings and confusion
- Join him by criticizing him for doing the same thing to you.

- ❑ Encourage him to report the behavior to her manager/supervisor.

7. You have complained on several occasions to your manager/supervisor about a team member who is involved in inappropriate behaviors, but she has not told you what actions have been taken to address the problem. What would you do?

- ❑ Keep complaining over and over until something is openly done about it.
- ❑ Complain to Human Resources that your manager/supervisor has refused to do something about your complaint.
- ❑ Trust that he has done something about it but realize that because of Human Resources policies your manager/supervisor cannot discuss with you the actions he has taken.
- ❑ Openly confront the team member yourself to put an end to the problems your manager/supervisor refused to address.

8. You have tried unsuccessfully on several occasions to get a promotion in your organization. What would you do to improve your chances of getting one the next time there is a vacancy?

- ❑ File an unfairness or discrimination complaint with Human Resources or the Equal Employment Opportunity office.

131

- ❏ Tell the hiring supervisor/manager how disappointed and angry you are about not getting the promotion.
- ❏ Ask your supervisor or the hiring manager what you can to do improve your chances of getting a promotion in the future.
- ❏ Write an anonymous letter to the president of the organization complaining about unfairness and discrimination in your department.

9. A conversation between you and a team member has escalated into an angry exchange. Both of you become very angry, and in the heat of the argument start making personal attacks, which neither of you really mean. What would you do to de-escalate and resolve the conflict?

- ❏ Walk away from the argument to show your displeasure with the other person's behavior.
- ❏ Apologize and demand an apology from the other person.
- ❏ Recommend that you both take a short 30-minute break before continuing the conversation.
- ❏ Stop talking for a moment, collect your thoughts, and restate your concerns calmly and precisely.

10. You urgently need to speak with someone who has not returned the last five telephone

voicemail messages you have left him during the past week. *What would you do?*

❑ Leave him one last message telling him that you don't appreciate his discourteous behavior refusing to return your telephone calls.

❑ Go by his office or contact another team member and find out if he has been out of the office for a few days.

❑ Complain to his manager about his refusal to return your urgent calls.

❑ Tell everyone on his team not to expect him to return telephone calls.

* The design of this quiz was influenced by the *Emotional Intelligence Quiz* in CRM Learning's Emotional Intelligence Participant Workbook (CRM Learning Video and Workbook Set, 2001): 3–5. This is the accompanying workbook to the Training Videotape with the same title: CRM Learning Video Training Set, *Emotional Intelligence.*

This book, *Emotional Intelligence in the Authentic and Diverse Workplace,* can be used as pre-reading material to the excellent CRM Learning Video and Workbook Training Set, *Emotional Intelligence* (2001).

The Emotional Intelligence Quiz
Answer Key

Please compare your answers on the quiz to the answer key below. Add the total number of points on the right hand column of your scoring sheet at the bottom of the page.

1. A = 5
    D = 10

    _____ points

2. C = 10

    _____ points

3. B = 10

    _____ points

4. B = 10
    C = 5

    _____ points

5. C = 10

    _____ points

6. A = 5
    B = 10

    _____ points

7. C = 10

    _____ points

8. C = 10

    _____ points

9. C = 10
    D = 5

    _____ points

10. B = 10

    _____ points

_____ Total Points

Understanding your Score

The objective of this quiz is to give you a general idea about your level of emotional intelligence. The highest score you can get is 100 points, and the average score is 50 points. Please discuss with your supervisor if you feel comfortable, or a partner or coworker, what your score means and what they can suggest you do to improve your level of emotional self-awareness and mastery to improve your emotional intelligence quotient.

Emotional Intelligence Profile

The beginning point of the process of developing emotional intelligences is self-awareness. This exercise is a starting point in assessing your level of emotional intelligence with regards to the core disciplines. On the scale below, moving from the left to the right column, please circle the number that best represents your current level with regard to each discipline.

From						To
Fearful and Distrustful	1	2	3	4	5	Trusting
Dishonest	1	2	3	4	5	Truthful
Disrespectful	1	2	3	4	5	Respectful
Unfair	1	2	3	4	5	Fair
Closed Minded	1	2	3	4	5	Open Minded
Unforgiving	1	2	3	4	5	Forgiving
Inconsiderate	1	2	3	4	5	Considerate
Unreliable	1	2	3	4	5	Reliable
Intolerant	1	2	3	4	5	Accepting
Uncaring	1	2	3	4	5	Caring
Blaming	1	2	3	4	5	Accountable
Rigid	1	2	3	4	5	Flexible
Untruthful	1	2	3	4	5	Truthful

Notes:_____
_____
_____
_____
_____

Review your responses after you have completed the exercise. Note the areas of your strengths; these are the areas that have the highest numbers. Also note the areas with the lowest numbers because these attributes represent the areas with the greatest potential for emotional growth and development. In your quest for developing emotional intelligence, they are essential for success in a diverse workplace.

For a further challenge, ask someone who knows you well to rate you on this scale. Discuss with them the similarities and differences you find. Don't try to resolve the differences; just learn the reasons they rate you as they do and think about the reasons you rate yourself as you did.

Behavioral Coaching Process

1. Identify one critical behavior that you would like to change that would foster greater levels of performance effectiveness and foster trust and collaboration at work.
2. Complete the Personal Commitment Contract and sign it.
3. Complete the section on Action Plans.
4. Select a coworker who works closely with you whom you believe is gifted in this behavior and ask the person if he would serve as your behavioral coach; share the behavioral coaching expectations with him.
5. Check with your coach on a monthly basis for feedback and guidance regarding the specific behavior you are committed to changing.

Tips for follow-ups with coach:

- Start the monthly conversation with the coach by reminding him of the behavior you are trying to change.

- Listen attentively to the feedback without interruption.

- If the feedback is negative, ask the coach what you could do differently to get the results you want.

- You may ask any follow-up questions pertaining to the feedback.

- Don't try to explain what happened, apologize, or appear defensive during or after the feedback.

- If the feedback is positive, ask for specific instance(s) when you were observed getting the behavior right. (The objective is for you to get as much specific information as possible and to help the coach become more observant of your behavior.)

- Say nothing else to the coach but "Thank you."

- Reaffirm your commitment to continue working on getting better at the new behavior.

6. After six months, request detailed feedback from your coach regarding your behavior during the previous six months.

7. After twelve months, ask your coach for a final briefing, requesting detailed feedback regarding your behavior during the previous twelve months.

8. Determine whether your behavior has changed.

9. If, after twelve months, you were unsuccessful at changing your behavior and still wish to keep working on changing it, you should seek professional help. Good luck!

Personal EI Commitment Contract

Take a few minutes to reflect on your behavior at work and identify one behavior that you would like to change; that if changed; would foster

_____

_____ (examples: *trust, respect, authentic relationships and collaboration, effective leadership).*

Then complete the Action Plan below and the Personal Commitment Contract.

■ One behavior that I would like to change is

_____

_____

■ I commit to doing everything within my power to change this behavior*

■ If I change this behavior, the benefits to me will be: (List three)

1.   _____

_____

2.   _____

_____

3. _____

   _____

Signature: _____

Date: _____

Witnessed By: _____

Date: _____

* Please refer to the Behavioral Coaching Process.

Conversation Questions

1. What are the benefits of emotional intelligence?

2. How does one develop emotional intelligence?

3. Why is it important to value commonalties in a diverse society?

4. What happens to us when we never forgive and never forget?

5. What happens to us when we never forgive but forget?

References and Suggested Reading

Blell, Denys and Kreisher, Robert D., "Effective Interpersonal Skills for Success in a Diverse Society," in, Austin, Marie A. *The Successful University Experience* (Kendal/Hunt 1999) 177–186.

Bracey, Hyler. *Building Trust* (Hyler Bracy 2002).

Bradberry, T & Jean Greaves. *Emotional Intelligence 2.0* (TalentSmart, 2009).

Buber, Martin. I and Thou (Scribner, 1970).

Capra, Fritjof. *The Web of Life* (Doubleday, 1996).

Caruso, David R. & Salovey, Peter. *The Emotionally Intelligent Manager* (2004).

Covey, Stephen M. R. *The Speed of Trust: The One Thing that Changes Everything* (Free Press, 2006).

Covey, Stephen R. *The 7 Habits of Highly Effective People* (Simon and Schuster, 1989).

Csikszentmihalyi, Mihaly. *Flow: The Psychology of Optimal Experience* (Harper and Row, 1990).

Druskat, Vanessa U., F. Sala, & G. Mount. *Linking Emotional Intelligence and Performance at Work* (Lawrence Erlbaum Associates, 2006)

Dyer, Wayne. *Your Sacred Self: Making the Decision to Be Free* (Harper and Row, 1995).

Frost, Peter J. *Toxic Emotions at Work* (Harvard, 2003).

Gershon, Michael D. *The Second Brain* (Harper Collins 1998)

Goleman, Daniel. Emotional Intelligence (Jossy-Bass, 1995).

Goleman, Daniel. *Social Intelligence* (Jossy-Bass, 2006).

Goleman, Daniel. *Working With Emotional Intelligence* (Jossy-Bass, 1998).

Greico, Mary Hayes. *The Nine Months Self-mastery Program Wholistic Psychology and Spiritual Healing* Training+*(See Mary Hays Greico's website for additional information regarding workshop.)*Jampolsky, Lee. *The Art of Trust* (Lee Jampolsky, 1994) 202–217.

Kaiser, Robert B. *"Outgrowing Sensitivities: The Deeper Work of Executive Development"* (Unpublished monograph presented at the Society for Industrial and Organizational Psychology, April 2002).

Krinsky, Leonard K., Kiefer, Sherman N., Carone, Pasquale A., and Yolles, Stanley F. *Stress and Productivity* (Human Sciences Press, 1984).

Lee, Blain. *Power Principle* (Simon and Schuster, 1996).

Leiberman, David J. *Instant Analysis* (St. Martin's Press, 1997).

Lombardo, Michael M. and Eichinger, Robert W. *FYI: For Your Improvement* (A Korn/Ferry Company, 2006).

Lundin, Stephen C., and James K. Arnold. *Personal Accountability: Your Path to a Rewarding Work Life* (Charthouse International Publication, 1997).

Luhmann, Niklas. *Trust and Power* (John Wiley, 1979).

McKay, Matthew, Peter Rogers, and Judith McKay. *When Anger Hurts* (MFJ Books, 1989).

Miller, John. *QBQ!: The Question Behind the Question* (Denver Press, 2004).

Miller, John. *Flipping the Switch* (Penguin, 2006).

Mintle, Linda, *Breaking Free From Anger & Unforgiveness* (Charisma House, 2002).

Moffitt, Phillip. *Forgiving the Unforgivable* (Life Balance Institute, 2002).

Pert, Candace, *Your Body is Your Subconscious Mind* (Sound True, 2000).

Pert, Candace. *Molecules of Emotions: Why You Feel the Way You Feel* (Scribner, 1997).

Pert, Candace. *Everything You Need to Know to Feel Go(o)d* (Hay House, 2007).

Reina, D.S., Michelle L. Reina, *Trust and Betrayal* (Berrett Koehler, 2006).

Robbins, Riki. *Betrayed!: How You Can Restore Sexual Trust and Rebuild Your Life* (Adams Media, 1998).

Ryan, Kathleen D. and Daniel K. Oestreich. *Driving Fear Out of the Workplace* (Jossey-bass, 1991).

Schlossberg, Nancy. "Marginality and Mattering: Key Issues in Building Community," in *Designing Campus Activities to Foster a Sense of Community*, Robert, Dennis C. (Jossey-Bass, 1989). Senge, Peter. *The 5th Discipline: The Art and Practice of the Learning Organization* (Doubleday, 1990).

Shaw, Robert Bruce. *Trust in the Balance* (Jossey-Bass, 1997).

Simon, George. *Working Together* (Crisp Books, 1989).

Smedes, Lewis B. *Forgive & Forget* (Pocket Books, 1984).

Tulgen, Bruce. *FAST Feedback* (HRD Press,1999).

Wall, Cynthia L. *The Courage to Trust* (New Harbinger, 2004).

Yerkes, Robert M. and John D. Dodson. "The Relationship of Strength of Stimulus to Rapidity of Habit-Formation," in *Journal of Comparative Neurology and Psychology*, 18 (1908).

Endnotes

FOREWORD

[1.] Leiberman, David J. *Instant Analysis* (St. Martin's Press, 1997), 280.

PREFACE

1. Emotional Intelligence: A term first coined by Daniel Goleman in *Emotional Intelligence* (Fireside, 1995) and subsequent works.

INTRODUCTION

1. Authentic Power: Blain Lee, *Power Principle* (1997) and Stephen R. Covey, *Principle-Centered Leadership* (1991). They both use the terms and concepts *coercive power*, *utility power,* and *principle-centered power* to describe what they call the "three paths to power" relative to leadership.

I use three similar terms and concepts in this book:
- *Coercive power*
- *Utility power*
- *Authentic power*

They represent the three types of systemic power that organizations generate. I also use Blain Lee's descriptions of the three types of leadership powers:
- *The power to do things to others*
- *The power to do things for others*
- *The power to do things with others*

to represent and describe the types of systemic powers (coercive, utility and authentic) and

149

capabilities that these organizations generate: 101–108

2. Coercive power: Blain Lee, *Power Principle*: 52–77

3. Coercive power: Blain Lee, *Power Principle,* 78–99

4. Self-mastery: Peter Senge, *The Fifth Discipline: The Art and Practice of the Learning Organization,* (1990): 139–173, uses the term *personal mastery* more broadly to encompass among other things "personal growth and learning." The term *self-mastery* is used in a somewhat limited way in this book. It represents emotional growth and professional development:

CHAPTER 1:
What is Emotional Intelligence?

1. The use of the term *emotional intelligence* in this book, is very similar to Daniel Goleman's, except that I have added two terms to the definition and concept: the ability to "express" your emotions and *impulse management.*

2. Also, the reference to "expressing emotions" is used differently from the way it is used in the book *When Anger Hurts,* by Matthew McKay, Peter Rogers, and Judith McKay. I use the term *express* to mean to verbally express yourself by saying you are angry instead of acting it out with an angry outburst. They discourage using the terms to discourage acting out our anger, with which I agree. When they recommend against expressing your emotions, what they

are actually discouraging is acting them out, not, I believe, verbal expression.

3. Social Intelligence: Goleman, Daniel, *Social Intelligence* (2006): the reference here is to social relationships and is very similar to Goleman's use of the term for how we relate interpersonally.

4. Network pattern: Fritjof Capra's definition of network systems is "a non-linear pattern that repeats itself." Capra, Fritjof in a presentation on *Sustainability: A Leadership Challenge,* during the System Thinker Conference in 1997; Fritjof, Capra, *The Web of Life* (Doubleday, 1996).

5. Social Intelligence: Another term coined by Daniel Goleman in *Social Intelligence* (Bantam Books 2006): 329–334; Buber, Martin, *I and Thou* (Scribner, 1970) 53–-168

6. Dyer, Wayne. *Your Sacred Self: Making the Decision to Be Free* (Harper, 1995):141, 157, 355–357

7. *Chasing the Snake*: This is an evocative story that motivational speaker and trainer John Miller tells his audiences (including his excellent training video The QBQ) that is reproduced in *Personal Accountability: Your Path to a Rewarding Work Life*, Lundin, Stephen C., and James K. Arnold (Charthouse International Publication 1997): 11–14

8. This a saying that is reported to have originated with Garrison Keillor sometime during the 1990s.

9. Post traumatic stress disorder and post traumatic stress syndrome: The use of theses terms in this book is similar to the way Wane Dyer uses them in *Your Sacred Self: Making the Decision to Be Free* (Harper, 1995): 11–14

10. Goleman, Daniel. *Emotional Intelligence: Why EQ Is More Important than IQ* (Bantam Books, 1995): 13–29

11. Pert, Candace. *Molecules of Emotions: Why You Feel the Way you Feel* (Scribner, 1997): 130–149: Goleman, Daniel. *Emotional Intelligence: Why EQ Is More Important than IQ* (Bantam Books, 1995):63

12. Covey, Stephen R. *The 7 Habits of Highly Effective People* (Simon and Schuster, 1989) 71–75

13. Senge, Peter. *The 5th Discipline: The Art and Practice of the Learning Organization* (Doubleday, 1990): 205–-232

14. Fake it till you make it: A concept in the Alcoholic Anonymous treatment program.

CHAPTER 2:
Forgive and Trust Unconditionally
1. Jampolsky, Lee. *The Art of Trust* (Lee Jampolsky, 1994): 121–123, 200–201.

2. Mintle, Linda. *Breaking Free From Anger & Unforgiveness* (Charisma House, 2002); Senge, Peter. *The 5th Discipline: The Art and Practice of the Learning Organization* (Doubleday, 1990): 300–301; Jampolsky, Lee. *The Art of Trust* (Lee Jampolsky, 1994):129, 200–201; Senge, Peter The *5th* Discipline, 300–-301.

3. Quoted by Dr. Humberto Negera, MD, Executive Director of the Carter Jenkins Center; author unknown.

4. Smedes, Lewis B. *Forgive & Forget* (Pocket Books, 1984): 73–123, 159–192.

5. Moffitt, Phillip. *Forgiving the Unforgivable* (Life Balance Institute, 2002): 2.

6. Moffitt, Phillip. *Forgiving the Unforgivable* (Life Balance Institute, 2002): 4.

7. Moffitt, Phillip. *Forgiving the Unforgivable* (Life Balance Institute, 2002): 5.

8. Jampolsky, Lee. *The Art of Trust* (Lee Jampolsky, 1994): 1–9; Dyer, Wayne. *Your Sacred Self: Making the Decision to Be Free* (Harper, 1995): 32, 167, 78, 117, 214, 229–230, 277, 300, 337; Kathleen D. Ryan and Daniel K. Oestreich. *Driving Fear out of the Workplace* (Jossey-Bass, 1998):129–167.

9. Trust: "Building Trust" describes four types of trust: *conditional trust, cooperative trust,*

negotiated trust, and *unconditional trust,* by Stuart Wells, in *Executive Excellence* (September, 1997): 11–12. In "Understanding the Four Levels of Trust," Terry Petra describes the four levels of trust as *situational trust, transactional trust, relationship trust,* and *loyalty,* in the *Fordyce Letter*, August 1, 2007: 2–-3; Niki Robbins describes in "The Four Stages of Trust" *perfect trust, devastated trust, restored trust.* The description goes on to describe the four types of restored trust as: *guarded trust, conditional trust, and selective trust,* in Robbins, Riki, *Betrayed!: How You Can Restore Sexual Trust and Rebuild Your Life* (Adams Media, 1998): 19, 39, 92, 153–158; Covey, Stephen M. R. *The Speed of Trust: The One Thing that Changes Everything* (Free Press, 2006): 43–123.

10. Luhmann, Niklas. *Trust and Power* (John Wiley 1979): 71–85, Shaw, Robert Bruce, *Trust in the Balance* (Jossey-Bass, 1997): 3–60; Dyer, Wayne. *Your Sacred Self: Making the Decision to Be Free* (Harper, 1995):167, 229–30; Luhmann, Niklas, *Trust and Power* (John Wiley 1979): 24–31, 39–47.

11. Kathleen D. Ryan and Daniel K. Oestreich, *Driving Fear out of the Workplace* (Jossey-Bass, 1998):17–33.

12. Distrust: Lewicki, Roy J. and Tomlinson, Edward C., in "Distrust," describes two types of distrust: *functional distrust* and

dysfunctional distrust. They also describe two levels of distrust: *violated distrust* and *tampering distrust*, ("Beyond Intractibility," *Org*, December 2003): 1–8

13. Stuart Wells. "Building Trust" in *Executive Excellence* (September 1997) 11–12; Robbins, Riki, "The Four Stages of Trust," in *Betrayed!: How You Can Restore Sexual Trust and Rebuild Your Life* (Adams Media, 1998): 122–125.

14. Stuart Wells. "Building Trust" in *Executive Excellence* (September 1997) 11; Robbins, Riki, "The Four Stages of Trust," in *Betrayed!: How You Can Restore Sexual Trust and Rebuild Your Life* (Adams Media 1998):122–125

CHAPTER 3:
Recognize Similarities and Value Commonalities
1. Blell, Denys and Kreisher, Robert D. "Beyond Diversity to Commonalities: The Movement Towards Valuing Commonalities as the Foundation of Community Building," In *University of South Florida Library Newsletter* (August 1999).

CHAPTER 4: Deal with Personal Prejudice
1. Schlossberg, Nancy, "Marginality and Mattering: Key Issues in Building Community," in *Designing Campus Activities to Foster a Sense of Community*, Robert, Dennis C. (Jossey-Bass, 1989): 5–15

2. Covey, Stephen R. *The 7 Habits of Highly Effective People* (1989): 235.

3. Simon, George, *Working Together* (1989): 5.

4. Luhmann, Niklas *Trust and Power* (John Wiley, 1979): 24–31.

5. Anton, William D., *What's in a Name?* (Revised August 2010). Reprinted here with permission.

6. Luhmann, Niklas, *Trust and Power* (John Wiley, 1979): 24–31.

CHAPTER 6: Build Relationships Across DIfferences

1. Capra, Fritjof in the presentation "Sustainability: A Leadership Challenge," The System Thinker Conference, 1997.

2. Ibid.

3. Buber, Martin, *I and Thou* (Charles Scribner, 1970): 53–168.

4. Blain Lee, *Power Principle* (1997): 101–108.

5. Senge, Peter, *The 5th Discipline: The Art and Practice of the Learning Organization* (Doubleday, 1990): 185, 375–376, 6–7, 68–69.

CHAPTER 7: Manage Differences Before They Become Conflict

1. Covey, Stephen R. *The 7 Habits of Highly*

Effective People (1989): 235.

CHAPTER 8: Do Your Best to Keep All Commitments
1. Senge, Peter, 218–224.

CHAPTER 9: Practice Personal Accountability

1. Miller, John. The "QBQ: The Question Behind the Question," in *Personal Accountability: Your Path to a Rewarding Work Life,* Lundin, Stephen C., and James K. Arnold (Charthouse International Publication, 1997): 11–14.

2. Ibid. 11–14; Miller, John *QBQ!: The Question Behind the Question* (Denver Press, 2004): 63.

CHAPTER 10: Be Fair with Yourself and Others
1. Lombardo, Michael M. and Eichinger, Robert W. *FYI: For your Improvement* (A Korn/Ferry Company, 2006): 141–145.

2. Cottinger, William "Managing Fairness" in *Executive Excellence*, (May 2000): 11–12.

3. Lombardo, Michael M. and Eichinger, Robert W. *FYI: For your Improvement* (A Korn/Ferry Company 2006): 141–145.

CHAPTER 11: Listen Carefully for Understanding
1. Wheatley, Margaret *Leadership and the New Sciences* (Barrett-Khoeler, 1992) 104–119

CHAPTER 12: Give and Receive Feedback with Care
1. Tulgen, Bruce. *FAST Feedback* (HR Press,1999).

CHAPTER 13: Be Flexible and Open to New Ideas
1. Jampolsky, Lee. *The Art of Trust* (Lee Jampolsky, 1994).

CHAPTER 14: Being Your Best at What You Do.
1. Heuerman, Tom, "Peak Performance," *The System Thinker*, Vol. 17, No. 3 (Pegasus Communication, 2006): 8–10.

2. Wells, Steve, "Achieving the Vision: The Psychology of Peak Performance" (unpublished paper, 2008): 1–4.

3. Csikszentmihalyi, Mihaly, *Flow: The Psychology of Optimal Experience* (1990):

4. Heuerman, Tom, "Peak Performance," *The System Thinker*, Vol. 17, No. 3 (Pegasus Communication, 2006): 8.

5. Ibid, 9.

6. Covey, Stephen R. *The 7 Habits of Highly Effective People* (1989); Heuerman, Tom, Ibid; Senge, Peter, *The 5th Discipline: The Art and Practice of the Learning Organization* (Doubleday, 1990).

7. Covey, Stephen R. *The 7 Habits of Highly Effective People* (1989): Yerkes, R. M., Dodson, J. D., "The relation of strength of stimulus to rapidity of habit-formation," *Journal of Comparative Neurology and Psychology,* 18 (1908): 459–482

8. Ibid.

9. Csikszentmihalyi, Mihaly, *Flow: The Psychology of Optimal Experience* (1990):

10. Heuerman, Tom, "Peak Performance," *The System Thinker,* Vol.17, No.3 (Pegasus Communication, 2006): 9.

11. Ibid.

12. Csikszentmihalyi, Mihaly, *Flow: The Psychology of Optimal Experience* (1990): Ibid.

EPILOGUE

1. Weisinger, Hendrie in *Anger at Work* (William Morow (1995).

2. Frost, Peter J. *Toxic Emotions at Work* (Harvard, 2003).

3. Krinsky, Leonard K. et. al., *Stress and Productivity* (Human Science Press, 1984).

4. Dyer, Wayne. *Your Sacred Self,* (Harper, 1995).

LaVergne, TN USA
15 March 2011
220230LV00001B/76/P